Enjoy!
Cal + Joan
Coolidge

Seventeen
Steps of Stone

Seventeen Steps of Stone

❧

Escaping Paradise

Cal Coolidge and Joan Coolidge

ISBN: 1544707002
ISBN-13: 9781544707006
Library of Congress Control Number: 2017904133
CreateSpace Independent Publishing Platform
North Charleston, South Carolina

This book is dedicated to our loyal dogs who were with us during this adventure: Abbie, Sally, and Peanut.

Contents

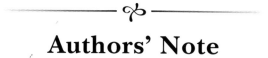

Authors' Note

THE FOLLOWING IS a true story, and although many of the names have been changed, the characters are real. Dialogue throughout is written as accurately as we can recall and is not intended as exact quotations. At times, we may speculate about what characters are thinking or reasons for their actions; those moments are totally our own impressions and may not reflect their motivations.

Foreword (Cal and Joan)

In 2006 and early 2007, we took a walk on the wild side. We did what dozens of people have told us they would love to do but lacked the nerve to try.

We left a comfortable life in the close-in suburbs of Washington, DC. We said goodbye to our home of fourteen years, respectable jobs, membership at the country club, and our beloved dog, Abbie, not to mention easy access to our two adult daughters, who were pursuing their own dreams on both coasts of the United States.

We bought a hotel on the Caribbean island of Saint Croix, one of the US Virgin Islands. Its name was the Pink Fancy Hotel, and its beauty could take your breath away.

This book tells our very true story of that entire experience. When we returned to a more conventional life, we were determined to write a book to share this adventure. Joan, as diligent as a librarian, set about the process in 2007, "before [she] could forget everything." Cal put completing the book on his bucket list, but as is his custom, he busied himself with resuming his hyperactive lifestyle. He knew he would "never forget anything." And he hasn't.

Several chapters are therefore based on Joan's memories and identified as such. Over the past ten years, Cal has had time to record and tell his stories many times, entertaining his pals on the golf course and elsewhere. His chapters are interposed with Joan's and pick up the story from about the time that reality set in.

We hope you enjoy the journey. Looking back, we've had nothing but fond memories of the entire experience, despite some close calls with disaster along the way. We loved the people we met on the island. Crucians have found a lifestyle that suits them just fine. What's not to love when you wake up every day far from the intensity and discord of modern-day America?

On Saint Croix, the bright sun shines every day, the daily shower inevitably produces a rainbow, and there is "always a breeze."

Prologue: The Rat (Joan)

SEVEN IN THE morning and time to get moving. I stretch in my bed. Cal, my husband of over thirty years, is always up long before me. The huge tropical room, decorated with brightly colored wallpaper and white wicker furniture, is deliciously cool from the window air conditioner, which runs all night, along with the ceiling fan, which is never turned off. Here I am, as they say, beginning another day in paradise.

Then I realize anew that I'm not on a tropical vacation. I live here! Everyone's dream, right? Chuck it all and move to an island in the tropics. Only there's more: not only am I not on vacation and live here, but we also work here. As in constantly, 24-7. The luxurious room I awoke in is part of a small, quaint, fourteen-room inn that we own! And although it's August—low season (which is apparently most of the year)—we do have a few guests. This is a bed-and-breakfast. I know that Cal will take care of setting up the meal, but I want to do my fair share.

I throw on a pair of gym shorts and a T-shirt. I know there's no point in showering at this time of day. First of all, our bathroom doesn't seem to want to deliver hot water until midday, after the solar panels have baked in the sun. Second, I know this is the only cool place in our two-room dwelling, so I will be sweating profusely the remainder of the day.

I reluctantly turn off the air conditioner for the day. It's far too expensive to run more than is absolutely necessary. I open the bedroom door to our adjoining den, home office, and linen storage—combined—all contained in about two hundred square feet. The blast of hot air takes my breath away. It is stiflingly hot on a Caribbean island in the summer. This is, of course, one of the many facts that hadn't even occurred to me as we'd charged headlong into this venture—that, along with the fact that Cal could sweat on the tundra.

I pass next into the open-air kitchen, where we set up the buffet breakfast for the guests. To call this kitchen small would be an understatement. Even to quote my mother and call it "a one-butt kitchen" is generous. It has maybe three feet by five feet of floor space. It has the necessary stove, refrigerator, and sink with no disposal, and there are lovely imported tiles on the counters, one of which opens onto the pool and serves as the buffet. But there are only five cupboards and only one drawer in which to store everything needed to serve the guests and ourselves, plus everything needed to prepare the food. Since it's open to the pool area, it always needs to be neat and clean, so everything needs to be stored some-how. The overflow finds its way to the all-purpose den. It had taken me days after the shipment of our household goods arrived to decide what the most important items to keep in the one-and-only drawer were. It ended up being silverware, which is what Cal had suggested from the start.

My first duty, and the highlight of my day, is to say good morning to Peanut and Sally. I sit on the floor with them, stroking them as their tails thump in happy greetings. They are both Crucian mutts. Sally is large and definitely part golden retriever, judging by the way she insists on constant attention. Peanut is small, with long hair, and is equally fond of attention. The girls, as we call them, came with the hotel, and I couldn't be happier about that.

Cal is up on a stool, cleaning the ceiling fan over the tiny kitchen that serves both our personal needs and is food-and-drink headquarters for what little we serve our guests in the way of breakfast and cocktails. It's probably the first time it's been turned off—let alone cleaned— in months, if not years. Ken, one of our few guests, is already sitting at a table by the pool with his laptop. Apparently, the wireless connection is actually working for a change. Climbing down from the stool, Cal suggests that he walk to the local bakery and pick up some pastries for the guests instead of setting out the usual breakfast. After he folds up the stepladder and leaves, trotting down the seventeen steps of stone that connect the main level of all things Pink Fancy to Prince Street below, I start to empty the dishwasher—no easy task, as once the its door is open, there's no room to walk around it to put the dishes away.

As I reach down for some plates, on the floor on the other side of the dishwasher and near the floor drain—exactly where Cal ten minutes ago had the stepladder positioned to clean the ceiling fan—I spot the biggest (not to mention ugliest) rat in the entire world. Cal had told me that he had had to dispose of several dead rats over the past month or so, most likely victims of our apparently enthusiastic (and efficient) ratter, Peanut. Fortunately, Cal's reported dead-rat finds had always occurred before the guests or I had made an appearance. Someone who'd lived on the island for many years had told us that "the rats own this island," so we weren't totally surprised that this was happening. However, here I was, alone in my kitchen, looking down at a (thankfully) dead rat well over a foot long if you included the tail. I can't remember if I closed the dishwasher door or not, but I exited the kitchen to the pool area in record time. I also can't remember where my beloved dogs—Sally and our suspected rat killer, Peanut—were at that particular moment, but they sure weren't here protecting me.

I thought I could just hang out at the breakfast table until Cal returned, but unfortunately, at that moment, Ken decided to refill his coffee cup. If he approached the pot on the buffet counter, there was no way he was going to miss seeing the huge dead rat lying on the kitchen floor, the very kitchen in which his breakfast was prepared each morning. I took a deep breath, went back into the kitchen, and stood at the counter, making conversation with Ken while doing my best to block his view of the rat inches from my feet. I was fairly certain that it really was dead (I don't think rats play possum), but that didn't make me feel any more comfortable.

He finally went back to his table and computer, and I hightailed it back out of the kitchen. As soon as I saw Cal at the gate, I raced down the seventeen stone steps to announce the grim news as quietly as possible. I'm not sure he believed me, as he had been in that exact spot just a short while ago, cleaning the ceiling fan. His normally red face turned white when he saw the size of the monster on the floor. I made sure Ken was distracted while Cal found a large garbage bag, somehow maneuvered the gruesome corpse into it, and (I presume) took it down to the trash.

Upon his return, I was standing back in the kitchen, setting up breakfast. With tears in my eyes, I turned to him and said, "I want to go home."

Whose idea was this, anyway?

PART 1

The Escape from the Real World

CHAPTER 1

The Idea (Joan)

THE ANSWER TO the question of whose idea this was is a toss-up and source of debate. In November, I had had a long, wine-heavy conversation with my college room-mate, Debbie, who was now living in California and had married Cal's best friend at Bradley. We heard all about her fabulous trip sailing and snorkeling in the Caribbean, one of my favorite places to vacation. She and I then decided we should quit our jobs and move there to run a "cute little B and B." We spent a long time on the phone, which we sometimes do, as we are a country apart and don't see each other often enough. But I'm sure neither of us was really serious. It was just talk. People have those fantasies all the time.

Except Cal—and he only heard half of this conversation. Throw any wild idea for an adventure at him, and he's immediately "all in," as he says. So, although I wasn't serious when, after hanging up, I announced that we should buy a bed-and-breakfast and move to the Caribbean, he shot right out of the recliner and started searching online for available properties! Damn Internet.

CHAPTER 2

๛

The Internet Is a Dangerous Place! (Cal)

FUELED BY THE idea that Joan was actually dreaming about throwing it all in and moving to the Caribbean, my juices were flowing. After all, I was the fantasizer of the marriage. Had it finally worn off on Joan?

Google "Caribbean real estate hotels B and Bs for sale," and you'll instantly learn that there are a lot of people trying to get out of that business. But when you're excited, you rarely think of it that way.

My mind raced as I clicked on all that came up.

Wow. There's Jamaica...been there once. Warm, didn't encounter any trouble. The people seemed nice on that four-hour snorkeling trip off the Veendam, *a Holland America cruise liner. Ah!* "A four-room property overlooking Los Rios Bay. Owners' quarters included. $800,000."

Click.

Haven't been to Trinidad...but what is this? "Luxury small hotel, destination of celebrities. Buildings constructed by the Portuguese navy in 1563. Click here for further information." *Oh my gosh, we are talking a major investment here.* "Six million dollars, serious inquiries only, please." I am rarely serious. *Move on!*

4

Click.

Costa Rica isn't in the Caribbean. "Secluded in the rain forest, only seventy miles from the Guanacaste airport."

Click.

"Our passion can be your dream. We have poured our souls into Regna Castellano, but now circumstances require that we return to the States to care for aging parents." *Look at these views! The zero-line pool! Twelve individual cottages...they look nice. We could handle this.*

Click.

"Priced at our cost, less the thousands of hours we have lovingly put into our dream for only $1,250,000. Business growing annually as our reputation spreads as the best eco-friendly getaway in Central America. On-site restaurant developed by my husband's culinary talents." *Whoops!* That eliminates the Coolidges. This husband is known for eating great food, not preparing it, and Joan will admit to being functional but not overly creative in the kitchen. A restaurant is out!

Click.

Back to Jamaica...and what's this? "Three hundred fifty thousand dollars, overlooks bay with dock." These photos are great...Well, it is just an octagonal, two-story house, so maybe we aren't buying a B and B...For that price, maybe we could just move there and chill. Nice photo of the native fishermen at our dock, delivering lobsters they just pulled out of the bay. The fishermen have machetes hanging from their belts...fishermen need machetes?

My mind flashes to page three of the weekly *Fairfax Connection* newspaper, dateline August 2010: "FORMER ALEXANDRIA COUPLE FOUND DEAD IN JAMAICA." Let's keep looking.

Ooh! Saint Lucia? What's this? "Twenty-two-room hotel, perfectly positioned for the upcoming 2007 International Cricket Championships. $2.7 million."

The aerial photos were interesting, and the place was rather nicely positioned on a cliff. *Strange. I guess the guests walk in? There doesn't seem to be a parking lot. Doesn't George Foreman live on the island?* We did have a guide point out his home above Marigot Bay when we had taken a snorkeling trip in 2002. But it turned out to be one of those celebrity things you hear when vacationing near a high-dollar neighborhood. My experience is, most of those guides make up stories—about how yesterday, they had Brad and Angelina on their bus—to make the guests *ooh* and *ah* a bit more. Rarely true.

Click.

"Historic hotel. Fourteen rooms overlooking lovely Christiansted Harbor, Saint Croix, in the US Virgin Islands, winter home to writers and playwrights." *Interesting.*

There must be fifty places taking my tropical imagination from Barbados to Saint Maarten (Dutch or French). Costa Rica...let's look at that one again. I've heard some good things about Americans moving there...although there was that ugly robbery-at-knifepoint thing Joan's cousin Liz went through.

Click.

New Zealand! How in the world did I get there? Interesting! "An eight-room villa perched on a vast open range. $1.9 million."

Cheap entertainment, this Internet island-hopping.

CHAPTER 3

The Idea, Continued (Joan)

FOR THE RECORD, I did make it clear that I wasn't serious, but like many people, Cal suffers from selective hearing. Sometime in December, he'd shown me several possible properties. To keep from repeating myself, I feigned interest but pointed out that I wouldn't even consider a non-English-speaking island, as we are both hopeless at any other language. He seemed to agree and therefore put the property he'd found in Costa Rica at the end of the list. This encouraged me to believe I was finally getting through to him and that maybe, I could yet convince him that I was serious about *not* doing this at all. So I went further and stated I didn't think I would want to go through all the hassle and red tape that was most likely involved in moving to a foreign country. Again, he seemed amenable to this opinion, and I grew even more hopeful that he would drop the whole idea. No such luck.

I think he may have anticipated my objections and planned to let me think I was winning the argument— and then pounce. And he did. After agreeing with me that those were two very valid points, he showed me his real goal: a very cute, quaint, small hotel on Saint

Croix—one of the US Virgin Islands. It's a US territory; the people speak English, use US currency, and are US citizens. So much for my objections now.

I was still not convinced that "my idea" was a good one. I decided to let the subject drop for the time being. After all, there were the holidays to enjoy, always a busy time, and we were both busy with jobs and life in general. Maybe this would just go away.

It didn't.

In January, I learned that Cal had been in contact, numerous times, not only with the real estate agent who had listed the property but even with the current owners. He was getting more and more enamored with this idea. He showed me all the information, the website, the correspondence, and so forth. He was anxious to make a trip to the island "just to take a look." I admit, I've never been one to pass up a cruise or trip to the Caribbean. So I agreed we could go for a week in February "just to look." I know that I stipulated on numerous occasions and in every way possible that this was going to be just a vacation, and we were not going to buy anything. My ever-optimistic husband just smiled and asked me to keep an open mind.

Researching the Historic Pink Fancy (Cal)

PHOTOS WERE VERY scarce on the website for the property that I was interested in. Apparently, the owners were very slow to embrace the technology that was revolutionizing advertising and the flow of information early in the new millennium. The website had a cute pencil sketch of the colonial-appearing main building, a series of palms blowing in the promised constant breeze coming off the adjacent spectacular Christiansted Harbor.

Google Earth showed me that *adjacent* really meant "close by," with a few buildings and one corner to turn past before a pedestrian could reach the boardwalk that started right at the seaplane terminal and extended all the way over at the huge yellow fort that was part of the National Park System. In between was a series of hotels that were probably much bigger than the four-building, fourteen-room Pink Fancy, as well as open-air restaurants and curio shops aimed at the tourist trade along the waterfront.

I asked the real estate agent who had placed the interesting ad, for some background information about the property. Her name was Mary, and she sent me a romantic description that further lit my fire of interest:

> Meticulously restored and listed on the National Register of Historic Places, the Pink Fancy Hotel is a romantic blend of our bygone plantation era with the sophisticated cachet of the inn's founder.
>
> It was in 1948 when Jane Winton Gottlieb, an actress and former dancer with the Ziegfeld Follies, opened the doors of a small Caribbean lodging, her Pink Fancy, to its first guests. Writers, artists, and the theatrical people from her sophisticated world were drawn to this charming spot, including playwright Noel Coward.
>
> Turning to writing in the 1950s, Gottlieb wrote historical novels of intrigue like *Passion is the Gale: Temptation and Torment in the Tropics*, no doubt set in a town very much like colonial Christiansted.
>
> Just as Jane Gottlieb was, guests of the Pink Fancy hotel became immersed in the intriguing history of the West Indies just outside their door. The oldest part of the four-building inn was constructed in 1780, when the young seafront town of Christiansted was the bustling capital of the Danish West Indies.
>
> Sugar and cotton plantations dominated island life then, the economy boomed, and merchants with family and trade ties to Europe

and America built elegant townhouses of yellow Danish brick and granite stones that came to the island on sailing ships as ballast.

Where Prince Street meets Strand Street, the jewel of a building now known as the Pink Fancy became a private club for wealthy planters. Those who gathered remembered, no doubt, the impoverished but impressive young clerk Alexander Hamilton, who left the island to be educated in New York in 1773. After joining the revolution, he served General George Washington, rose to become America's first Secretary of the Treasury— and is still spoken of often in Christiansted.

By the midnineteenth century, king sugar was dethroned by the abolition of slavery and by the development of sugar beets that could be grown in cooler climates. Saint Croix settled into a sleepy existence under the sun, all but forgotten by the world until March 31, 1917. That day, the United States, seeking a stronger Caribbean presence for national security, purchased the Danish West Indies for $25 million in gold.

After World War II, with the development of jet aircraft, Saint Croix saw an influx of "continentals" from the mainland, delighted to vacation in America's paradise.

Some, like Jane Gottlieb, chose to begin new lives here and help restore the charming colonial town. The Saint Croix Landmarks League swung into action in 1948, the year the Pink Fancy's doors opened. Its members fought to preserve the Christiansted Historical Site, an open-air treasure now under the auspices of the National Park Service.

And so, along with its historic setting, the Pink Fancy has been preserved for your delight as one of the last remaining historic Caribbean inns. This small, unique hotel is a living symbol of Saint Croix's golden age, the late-eighteenth and nineteenth centuries, when sugar was king— as well as the island's rebirth under the American flag.

Wow, I thought after reading this. *I have found a gem.*

CHAPTER 5

It Wasn't Because (Cal)

MAKING A DECISION to buy a hotel in the Caribbean requires the ability to think outside the box. This is something I have never had trouble with. However, trouble has occasionally found me due to this skill. In fact, in keeping with my lifelong observation that people's strengths are almost always their weaknesses as well, my out-of-the-box mind has gotten me to where I am…for better or worse.

A willingness to take risks is also a requirement. There are multiple sides to risk taking. Considering the phases of life and what must be given up to take a different course should always be a factor. The potential reward of taking on a new endeavor should be a motivator as much as the adventure of it all. (Are you listening?)

Then why, you ask, did we, a couple with thirty-plus comfortable years living the corporate life in a nice neighborhood, members of a country club and pseudomembers of the Catholic Church, suddenly set a new course?

It wasn't without some analysis; it wasn't with complete knowledge, either.

It may have been a time-of-life thing. It may have been easier for me to internally justify making such a drastic move with its apparent benefits and rewards (minimizing the apparent risks) than to prepare myself for a "normal" retirement. I've rarely been seen as "normal."

It wasn't because, ever since our wedding on a cold, foggy December day in 1974 in Metamora, Illinois—when one of the songs for the service was "Follow Me," by John Denver—Joan had made a life of following me, all the while being the rock that kept us grounded.

Follow me where I go, what I do, and who I know
Make it part of you to be part of me
Follow me up and down all the way and all around
Take my hand and say you'll follow me.

We were comfortably settled in a nice house that Joan had made into an even nicer home in a wonderful neighborhood, just six miles from the self-proclaimed most important city in the free world. It was the home in which we had raised our girls.

During the first fifteen years of our marriage, Joan had followed me on moves from Illinois to North Dakota, Texas, Michigan, Virginia, back to Texas, and then back to Virginia. She had had more than the right to say "enough already." I knew she wouldn't.

It was, after all, her idea that she would "just move to the islands and buy a B and B." It's a fact she attempts to deny, but it was she, in a slightly compromised state of mind, who actually first suggested it. That actually did happen. At the time, the question was, would she tell me where? And the second question was, would she invite me to follow her?

I have always had an extreme case of optimism. I also remember being aware of impending dangerous circumstances at an early age and learning to extract myself from developing trouble. My longtime mentor, Sherel, during my career at Texas Instruments, had often told me, "I love watching you wade out among the alligators and then work your way out of the swamp."

Never afraid of the unknown, I too often relied on my ability to act off script with the best of them. In fact, I may not possess the risk-aversion gene. I've taken a few beatings as a result but somehow always thought the experience was worth it and that the stories of those failures were entertaining and worth telling. Most people likely try to forget their mess-ups. Not me.

Take, for instance, our venture into horse racing in the late 1990s. My interest in it got started when I tagged along with some colorful characters like Nick and Joe, whom I'd met while living in Dallas. They taught me a bit about betting on horses for recreation and the thrill you get when you pick a ten-dollar trifecta correctly and, two minutes later, cash a ticket for $1160. Just remember—that is all for entertainment, not a way to make a living—and it's really not a way you want to lose a living.

On a cruise with the girls over the turn of the millennium, I took the bait and bid on a "horse" that was actually a stick pony that, after we participated in all the cruise director's antics throughout the week, was to compete in the Kentucky Derby, a dice-rolling game that moves the horses along a board until one wins. All the money that had been bid to "own" these steeds was now in the pot, awaiting the winner.

The cruise director was the typical ham who, on that race day, worked the crowd into a frenzy by doing interviews with the owners and jockeys before a last-minute "drug test" of one of the horses just prior to the race. To administer the test, the cruise director took the selected pony behind a white sheet and collected a "urine sample" to the sound of a four-inch faucet being let open. This had the crowd in hysterics. But when he emerged with a beaker of pineapple juice from around the corner, holding it up to the light and dipping an alkaline strip for testing pool water into it, no one was prepared for what he did next. After looking unsuccessfully for a place to pour the sample out, he shrugged and drank the liquid down. This drew shrieks of disgust from the ladies and belly-busting laughter from most of the guys.

The race began, and with each roll of the dice, our number-four horse, SilverDaysCharm (named in honor of our twenty-fifth anniversary), took a commanding lead and managed to reach the last square before the finish line, well ahead of his seven opponents. There was $860 on the line with one more roll of a four. My heart was beating at about 160 beats per minute until the damn number-three horse came charging up with two sets of doubles to nose us out. *Oh my God*, I thought, *if I can get that kind of rush from a stick-horse race, I have to try my hand at the real thing.*

This led to participating in five or six thoroughbred partnerships in Maryland and later with Dogwood Stables out of South Carolina. We had a few winners but came nowhere near breaking even on those ventures. They did provide the kind of adventure I seem to need in my life, but I was cured of that little dream after it ate the first $50,000.

Once I began dreaming the dream of owning a hotel in the Caribbean, though, it seemed to feed my ever-optimistic brain.

Joan had been an education major at Bradley University, where we met in 1973. The series of geographic moves I made during my career at Texas Instruments didn't allow her the opportunity to pursue a serious career outside the home. She taught for two years (1977 and 1978) in the Catholic schools in East Dallas and worked a series of summer jobs. Then Melinda was born in February 1981, and Joan dedicated herself to raising our girls for the next eighteen years.

Eventually, the girls successfully launched their own lives. Both Melinda and Sarah were ambitious, smart, and pursuing challenging futures. Melinda, a Tufts magna cum-laude graduate with a double major in international relations and French, was in her second year at Georgetown Law School after working for a couple of years in the nonprofit world for Public Citizen, which is rooted in Ralph Nader's consumer-protection philosophy. She had also found her life partner in David, an impressive second-generation Korean American, political activist, and strategist who never slept, it seemed—unless, of course, I expected him to come along on a hike before noon at our vacation home at the Homestead in Hot Springs, Virginia. Drove me nuts!

Sarah, our career student, had walked away from an academic scholarship at Emory University in Atlanta after one semester to transfer to the most expensive (for an out-of-state student) philosophy program in Ann Arbor, Michigan. We couldn't complain, however: she knocked out four years in three, graduating at the top of her class and earning the Frankena Prize as the top philosophy grad. But why stop there? She was on to UCLA for her PhD with a full ride and a stipend for teaching as a graduate assistant.

So, with self-sufficient kids, we were not needed as a safety net. Why not buy a hotel in the Caribbean? Wouldn't you?

My main career had burned out early after twenty-six years. The last eight, I had been at the executive level at Texas Instruments Defense Systems and laterTRW Space Systems Groups, both two-billion-dollar businesses. I had been a victim of mergers and acquisitions and had had a big mouth around new management (see "no fear of risk," above).

I had probably been well suited for my second career as a financial advisor at Smith Barney. It could be lucrative, but it was nothing I took overly seriously. I had been lucky in my aerospace-electronics career with stock options and bonuses during the late-nineties dot-com boom. I had remembered to sell high…mostly.

Well, money never seemed to motivate me after that good fortune. That certainly must have frustrated my managers at Smith Barney, as nothing *but* money seemed to motivate them. It's a reasonable philosophy when you're managing money, but it was starkly different from my experience interfacing with senior military officers and defense-business executives who, at least in the eighties and early nineties, still thought of their professions as duty versus an opportunity to cash in.

While money did not motivate me to work harder, my parents had instilled in me a sense of practical finance. Mom was frugal, as most Depression-era children learned to be, but she also knew the value of living well. Compared to my siblings, I missed the frugal lesson and got a double dose of the living-well pill. My family seemed to see me as living large, with more fun on my calendar than some in that New England Yankee clan were ever comfortable with.

I had, however, been obsessed with funding my retirement savings at every opportunity and always to the legal limit. Even with my career cut short by the mergers, consolidations, and just plain getting fired for being different at TRW, I had managed to put away almost enough from deferred compensation and in 401(k)s to make it from age forty-nine to eternity—if I didn't screw it up!

While I loved the risk that came with ventures that friends presented to me that realistically had no chance—and that series of horse-racing partnerships that had even less—they did provide a thrill and got my heart rate up as we watched Jerome Park fade in the stretch and finish fourth at Pimlico.

It took me a while to believe what you've probably heard about horse racing and many other risky ventures: "If you want to make a little money in that business, start with a lot of money." I preferred lines such as this one, which implies that racing is a game for optimists: "No one ever committed suicide with an unraced two-year-old in the barn."

For us, it was important for something as speculative as a Caribbean hotel to work without affecting our retirement savings. That meant coming up with over a million from nonretirement assets or loans. That was the kind of challenge I loved.

We had watched the local real estate market go up in the greater Washington, DC, area to a level that no longer made sense. Why, in 2005, were people snatching up smallish homes built in 1953 with one-car garages in Alexandria for prices pushing $800,000?

We had paid $340,000 in 1992, and that had seemed over the top then. In a nice neighborhood along the Potomac, only seven miles from the Pentagon and Memorial Bridge, these places had sold for less than

$40,000 when built in the early fifties. The bubble bothered me. I repeatedly suggested to Joan that we should cash in. We had considered some downsizing options locally, but nothing turned us on or really offered us the chance to buy for substantially less.

Why bunt when you can swing for the fences?

CHAPTER 6

— ✌ —

The Trip (Joan)

I WILL ADMIT that I was excited, as I always am, about a vacation in the Caribbean. And, of course, that's all it was: "just a vacation." The flight took about six hours: three from Washington, DC, to Miami and three more from Miami to Saint Croix. Our conversation was animated speculation on his part and caution on mine—that's not all that unusual, actually.

Saint Croix is the largest of the US Virgin Islands. It's located forty miles from Saint Thomas and Saint John. After being there for a while, I got an impression from the locals that there's competition among the three islands for tourist dollars—and perhaps some jealousy—with Saint Croix perpetually in third place. The capital of the USVI was once on Saint Croix, just four blocks from the hotel we were flying toward, but at some point, it was moved to Saint Thomas. To hear some Crucians tell it, they're always getting the short end of the stick from the government, tourist association, and so on. And this certainly may be true. But after a while, I also realized that it cost more and was harder to get to. It's farther away, and there are virtually no direct flights, so it's really not easiest for tourists.

After landing, we took a cab to our destination on the other side of the island: the Pink Fancy Hotel. This was one island we had never visited (possibly due to the reasons mentioned above), so we took in all the sights we could during the drive. The cab driver was listening to a very loud sermon with a lot of alleluias on the radio, but he did point out a few things on the way. As we drove—on the left side of the road, by the way—into Christiansted, I fell in love with the colorful, old architecture. Saint Croix has been under the flags of six different countries: France, Spain, England, the Knights of Malta, Denmark, and the United States. I believe that most of the buildings in Christiansted date from the late eighteenth century, including the Pink Fancy, which has a historical marker placing it at 1780. I would say there are fewer palm trees here than on some other Caribbean islands, but aside from that, it definitely made me feel the magic of the tropics.

When we pulled up to the hotel, I really didn't notice the surroundings all that much. Most Caribbean-island neighborhoods seesaw from run-down to quaint to colorful to extravagant and back again, over and over. There are the areas to which the tourists gravitate, usually near the water; areas where the wealthy have built huge vacation or full-time homes with spectacular views; and areas where most of the working-class locals humbly live. There was a vacant lot across the street, where some ambitious entrepreneur was attempting to start a rental-car business with a tent apparently serving as an office. Farther down the street was a barbershop and a rather run-down-looking convenience store. Past them, where the street ended, we later learned, there was low-income housing that looked adequately maintained. But I was mostly paying attention to the hotel. It was walled and gated, so from the street, all I could see was the main building and its lower, street-level rooms. It was painted a pale, Caribbean blue with bright-pink trim and wonderfully colorful hurricane shutters topped by a pink, corrugated-metal roof. Across the front of the second floor were the six flags of the various countries of the island's past and present. It was impressive.

We unloaded our luggage from the cab and rang the bell. Dora, one of the owners, came down the seventeen ancient stone steps, which we later learned had originally served as ballast in Danish ships, and greeted us. Sally and Peanut, the hotel dogs, were at the top of the steps, wagging their tails. Although Dora and Cal had been in e-mail and phone contact, I had not been involved, so this was my first encounter with her. She seemed quite pleasant and friendly, but then, she was not only the owner and hostess of the Pink Fancy, she was also trying to sell it to us. I did soon discover that she was pleasant and friendly to all of the guests—which was to be expected.

Dora pointed out the historical marker that designated the property as on the National Register of Historic Places. We then climbed for the first time, the seventeen steps of stone to the main level, where Sally and Peanut did their job and greeted us happily. Being a huge animal lover, I enjoyed giving them the attention they so obviously expected. When I finished my dog duties, I straightened up, looked around, and, I will admit it, fell instantly in love.

Sally and Peanut, the Hotel Dogs

The Pink Fancy was as charming a place as any I had previously discovered in the Caribbean. We were standing on a beautiful tile patio, in the center of which was a lovely pool. The main building, of which we had seen the back from street level, was to our right. It had four beautiful rooms on this level and four modest rooms downstairs, separately fenced and gated. Behind us was "the schoolhouse," painted blue, which held the kitchen, office, and owner's residence. There was a large awning off the open-air kitchen, under which were situated a patio table and six chairs for serving breakfast. To our left was a little yellow building, which held one of the more modest rooms. Out of our sight behind the schoolhouse was the "cottage up the hill," painted orange with blue shutters, which held two more wonderful rooms. It had its own porch in front and a large patio to the side. All of the windows on all of the buildings had colorful hurricane shutters. There was a bright-blue wall to the left of the pool that displayed colorful works of Caribbean-themed "oil-drum art." A winding staircase led up to a first deck big enough to hold four lounge chairs, which would be perfect for sun-worshipping guests. More winding stairs led to a second, covered patio, from which the water of Christiansted Harbor was visible. You could see even Saint Thomas and Saint John in the distance. This was fabulous. I could imagine serving rum drinks to guests as they marveled at the view.

There were jungle-like gardens to the left of the schoolhouse and between the schoolhouse and the two-room cottage up the hill. They were filled with exotic plants, a huge actively producing mango tree, and various palm trees and tiled walkways. The whole complex was unique, charming, and exotic, and it filled me with happiness to just be there.

Dora's partner Spike (whose name was actually Stephanie, which we didn't know until we saw the closing papers), the other owner, took charge of checking us in. Although we were potential buyers, we were also paying guests. We were slightly taken aback and a little amused by her method of check-in. In her German accent, she curtly went over the "rules." Most of these were within the realm of normal and understandable, such as no diving into the shallow pool. But when she quite sternly informed us, as she did all guests, that breakfast was served "between eight thirty and nine thirty, not a minute before and not a minute after," we didn't feel exactly welcome. When she showed us to our room, she made a great point of informing us that she had upgraded us from a modest room to the deluxe room named "Upper Love." Why did I feel that she expected profuse gratitude?

The room was beautiful and became my favorite in the hotel. It was quite large, with bright-yellow walls and a king-size, four-poster antique bed. There was a sitting area with a marble-topped antique table, along with a couch and two chairs, two antique dressers, and a gorgeous chandelier. All of the rooms had somewhat dated kitchenettes, each with a small refrigerator, sink, and two-burner stove. The bathroom was also quite large, with white tile everywhere. The floor was dark Brazilian walnut.

We were learning quite quickly that Spike could be rather pushy, to put it mildly. After we unpacked and settled in, we went back to the patio table to get acquainted with these ladies and decide our schedule for the week. We wanted to get to know the island and what it had to offer, along with learning everything we could about the property. (I still had no intention of even considering buying the hotel, but I was more than willing to enjoy my week.) As an experienced tour director in her native Munich in a former life, Spike had all the information at hand on what activities were available. But, unlike any concierge I've ever dealt with, she also was adamant about what we should do and the order in which we should do it.

After much discussion, we finally acquiesced to her itinerary, both of us wondering, *Whose vacation is this, anyway?* At the suggestion of our hosts, we walked to have dinner at a nearby restaurant serving local cuisine. It was wonderful (especially the rum punches). The next morning, we boarded an open-air bus for a tour of the island. Sweeney was our driver and our guide. Unfortunately for him, we were the only passengers. We felt bad, as we knew our fee wouldn't even cover the gas. Maybe what we should have wondered was *why* we were the only passengers. This was February, after all: high season. Where were all the tourists? However, Sweeney was such a wonderful, informative guide that those thoughts never crossed our minds.

Our first stop was the botanical gardens, which were lovely, and he knew all kinds of fascinating facts about the local flora. Next was Whim Plantation. At one time, the island had been divided into 150 sugar plantations. Many ruined stone windmills that were once used for separating the molasses from the cane dotted the island.

Whim had a plantation-house tour, and then Sweeney walked with us to the ruins and entertained us with more interesting historical facts. We then drove on to the Cruzan rum factory for a short tour and tasting. A stop for lunch in Fredericksted, the other town on the island—on its west end—showed us a beautiful, newly renovated pier and lovely beaches. It started raining before we left, which was appropriate, as the next and final part of the tour was a drive through the rain forest.

We tried to stop at a bar there that was famous for its beer-drinking pig, but we found out that they didn't let the pig drink beer when it was raining. I guess they were afraid he'd get drunk and slip on the wet earth. (I later learned that they actually now serve the pig alcohol-free beer. Apparently, there was a liver problem involved in this decision.) All in all, it was a good overview of the island, and we had lots of fun. It was exactly what we like to do on vacation. Spike had been right after all.

We spent the next few days walking along the boardwalk, having great meals, renting a car, and going to beaches—all the things tourists do. We took a half-day trip to Buck Island, a national park established by John F. Kennedy. Buck Island has been named one of the hundred most beautiful beaches in the world by *National Geographic* and has an underwater snorkeling trail. The shops we stopped into were typical of Caribbean islands—very nice ones selling jewelry and souvenirs. The beaches were perfect and not too crowded. In fact, one of the things I liked best about the island was that it wasn't packed with tourists. The cruise ships didn't stop there, so you were not trying to tour and shop with five thousand of your closest friends. In retrospect, this might have been our second clue that tourism as a profitable industry was struggling on this island.

When we weren't taking in the sights or relaxing on the beach, we were learning as much as we could about the property itself. Dora seemed happy to show us around and explain how things worked. We learned that the hotel had three cisterns. Two of them were freshwater and were used for showers, drinking, and so on. The third was gray water, which was for toilets and the yard. Dora mentioned that they could also tap into city water (which is desalinated), but that they'd never had to, as the cisterns had never run dry. Water is a commodity on an island and quite expensive—as is, we learned later, electricity and just about everything else. We were very impressed with the cisterns, the solar-powered water heater, and the breakfast setup. We heard, for the first of many times, "It's easy!"—about everything.

Dora showed us various rooms as guests checked out, but never those that were occupied. One thing that struck me as rather odd from the very beginning was the owners' reluctance (refusal, actually) to show us the rooms in the schoolhouse. These consisted of their own living quarters, the office, and the kitchen. I can't imagine ever buying a home with only a five-minute inspection, but that's basically what they were demanding. I failed to pick up on several red flags during the week.

Cal Coolidge and Joan Coolidge

We spent one day with Mary, the seller's real estate agent. Cal had been in contact with her several times prior to our arrival and had arranged to have her show us other available small hotels and B and Bs. She was also becoming our real estate agent—and good friend.

We looked at another property for sale called the Palms at Pelican Cove, which had a lower price than the Pink Fancy, but it also needed some work. To my mind, at this point, the Pink Fancy was perfect in every way and needed no improvements! Cosmetically, it seemed perfect.

Mary drove us around parts of the island that hadn't been covered on the bus tour, and we saw some beautiful sights and very impressive homes in the hills. She pointed out a castle of sorts owned by the "Contessa," which was perched high up on a hill on the east end of the island, affording views of both the Atlantic Ocean and the Caribbean Sea.

With each passing day, we were actually more into the idea of making an offer on the hotel. We talked about nothing else. We discussed all of the ramifications of such a move—or so we thought. On Wednesday, as we were sitting at lunch at Rum Runners, our new favorite restaurant on the boardwalk, we looked at each other and asked simultaneously, "Are we nuts?"

CHAPTER 7

❦

The Deal (Joan)

THE ANSWER WAS a resounding yes, apparently, because we decided to make an offer. We really did feel that we had thought this through thoroughly, and although we knew it was a wild and crazy idea, it was doable. We knew it would be a huge step and change in our lives. We did realize it was slightly unorthodox, to put it mildly. But we were caught up in the excitement of a complete change in lifestyle. Quite a few people over the next six months or so would ask us this question: "Is this something you've both dreamed of doing all of your lives?" I think that that is the question we should have asked ourselves from the beginning, because the answer was—no! We hadn't been dreaming about or planning this for years. We had just come up with the idea in the spur of the moment and talked ourselves into it.

After two days of offers and counteroffers, meetings with Mary, and one-on-ones with the sellers, mostly Dora, we had a signed contract. This also happened to be on my birthday, Friday, February 10. It was also the night of the Valentine's Day jump-up in Christiansted.

Mocko Jumbies on the streets of Christiansted at Jump-Up

Jump-ups are glorious, colorful street parties that happen four times a year. (Carnival, just after Christmas, is a much larger celebration.) At jump-ups, there are food and drink vendors set up on all of the streets, which are closed to vehicles. There are musicians spread out at various points, both individuals and groups, and steel-drum bands galore. My favorite was a group of schoolchildren. And most essential to any jump-up are the mocko jumbies. A mocko jumbie is originally from African culture. It is ten to twenty feet high, dressed very colorfully in what we would think of as plaid pajamas, and wears a mask. The artists who play them—many are children—are on stilts, performing unbelievable dance moves while towering above the crowd. Their traditional role is to keep the evil spirits away from the village and the parade. They have been a part of island culture for over two hundred years and have existed in Africa as early as the thirteenth century.

Before Cal and I left to experience our first jump-up on our new island home, Spike and Dora presented me with a birthday rum cake and gave me a mocko-jumbie wall hanging. The hotel guests who were present joined in singing "Happy Birthday" to me. It was all very festive, and the other guests asked Cal how he would top this on my next birthday. We then called our daughters to tell them the big news. They, of course, knew we had been considering this move. I think they had been sure we wouldn't actually do it. But when we revealed our decision, they were as supportive of us as we had always been with them. I'm fairly certain that they thought we were absolutely insane. We have very smart daughters.

CHAPTER 8

— ❧ —

Are We Serious? (Cal)

WE WERE SERIOUSLY considering buying a lovely small hotel on a Caribbean island. In fact, we'd signed a contract to buy the Pink Fancy. The contract did have conditions that could have allowed us an out, but we had taken the first steps to make it happen.

This likely would be the time when a more cautious and perhaps smarter guy would say to his partner, "Why don't we take a few weeks to think about this?" Oh, but I could see all the upsides and compartmentalize the down.

Certainly, we were underestimating the size of the bite we were thinking about taking. I had a habit of taking large bites. Sometimes you take one and then have to chew it—a piece of advice I had first heard as a young teen from an early mentor of mine: Mr. Megson. I am an aggressive eater!

Joan had a history of acting as the designated wet blanket on some of my small ideas and more than a few of my "I-wants," but she was always willing to take the challenge on the big ones. After all, she'd agreed to move first to Grand Forks, North Dakota, as a newlywed so that I could repay my ROTC obligation to the air force. After my short but brilliant career as a missile-launch officer and eight years with Texas Instruments, she'd agreed to leave bright-and-shiny Dallas in 1983 when I was offered a promotion to run Texas Instruments' Detroit office in what was likely-to-be-dreary Michigan.

In the end, she'd always yielded to me on the "big stuff."

The warm winter sun, the soft breeze, the rum, the views, the people, the feeling of freedom…it all plays on your mind. When you lack the fear-of-risk gene, there isn't much to hold you back.

The conversation Joan and I were having now was transitioning from "Why?" to "Why not?" In actual fact, there were no real *whys* being asked.

It was not just one thing that moved the conversation. It was an avalanche of optimism and our view of how things could be down here. We'd be getting away from the self-proclaimed most important city in the world, which can wear on you after fifteen years of kissing the asses of elected and appointed officials. It wasn't like I was still in some big-time defense-industry career any longer, hoping to one day be appointed secretary of the air force.

We'd be leaving some very lovable friends and neighbors, yes, but you learn that too many folks in the Washington area have a serious case of Potomac fever, honestly believing they are irreplaceable.

There was the very cynical thumb of the nose I would be giving to those still busy keeping America safe for democracy in the defense business and my new workmates who seemingly could think of little other than money and the financial markets with Smith Barney or the other Wall Street firms.

Living in Washington, we chuckled about how certain people were known to "tentatively accept" your invitation to dinner, a game, or some black-tie political event. We always knew they were holding out hope for a better offer—not the sincerest bunch you'd ever meet.

On the island, it was nothing like that. It was one human family, and everyone could just chill. "We are all here because we aren't all there," as the bumper sticker we saw on Saint Croix said. "Life in the left lane" was another way of putting it. We were loving the idea, and we had talked ourselves into being very serious.

CHAPTER 9

Moving Fast (Cal)

IT ALL HAPPENED fast.

Joan and I had moved for business five times over the past thirty-five years, and in situations like that, you have to make quick decisions. A three-day house-hunting trip was all you normally had. In this case, we should not have been pressured to make a quick decision, but we'd had practice—and if we returned home not having given it a shot...who knows? We probably wouldn't have taken this walk on the wild side.

It was Joan's birthday, as she noted—February 10— our sixth day on Saint Croix. In rapid succession, we'd made an offer, gotten a counteroffer, and countered again. The hoteliers accepted our counteroffer...and, oh my God, we owned a hotel! I had cut quite a few deals in my career, which probably made it all seem natural to me.

This, however, might have been the first deal that would totally change our lives. But today, it seemed it could only be for the better. It would certainly be exciting.

We could handle the disruption. There had already been plenty of those, with the abrupt ends of careers, five moves in four different states over thirty-two years, breast cancer for Joan, some major screw-ups by me (usually made while thinking I was bulletproof). We'd survived and were ready for more.

As our brash president at the time said, "Bring 'em on."

Getting everything lined up to take possession of a hotel fifteen hundred miles of ocean away was daunting—even besides the obvious hurdle of coming up with the purchase price of $1,195,000. It was a punch list I was made for. Among the tasks due in the next four months were these:

1. Make the escrow down payment before leaving the island.
2. Prepare to gather another million and change to complete the deal.
3. Exit the investment business (for me) and the school-library system (for Joan) gracefully, hoping somehow to keep the healthcare benefits they provided us (didn't happen).
4. Sell the house and whatever else we possessed on the mainland (we were not planning on coming back, you see).
5. Tell friends, colleagues, and family of the adventure we were about to take.
6. Start to market the hotel to assure a fast start financially.

The reaction when we told neighbors, friends, and especially relatives ranged from disbelief—as if we'd been selected for a one-way trip to Mars—to envy that we had the guts to try this to "This has always been our dream." You later learn that these things are all said with best wishes but impending doubt in everyone's minds.

What they may have meant to say was, "You must be nuts."

CHAPTER 10

Working the Task List (Cal)

FIVE OF THE six tasks were easier than I had imagined.

To be honest, when we sealed the deal, I had anticipated an escrow deposit of $20,000 to $25,000. Mary, the real estate broker representing both the seller and us, let us know that on the island, 10 or 20 percent was expected. In other words, in the six figures. Yikes! We cut a check off our taxable brokerage account for 10 percent. Fortunately, it didn't require us to sell any equities, but it got my attention.

You learn quickly that Crucian banks don't have much interest in small hotels as collateral, nor are they overly interested in any recent arrival to the island (as of last Saturday, in fact) inquiring about borrowing a million bucks. They were nice, if a bit surprised to talk with someone who was willing to make a decent investment on the island, but it became clear very quickly that we'd have to pay cash at closing. Our cash.

That obviously meant selling the house, liquidating a huge percentage of our nonretirement assets, and probably wiping out a big piece of our retirement savings.

The only alternative would be to find private financing somehow.

As soon as we returned to our Virginia home, I was dying to tell my colleagues at Citigroup Smith Barney, and my manager, Guy "the Knife" DeAndes, that I was flipping my nose at the investment business. I worked among a fun-loving bunch of good people, but one or two of them looked down on the newer ones with an arrogant, "better than thou" attitude. They had been around long enough to have a steady stream of more than $30,000 a month rolling in during both bull and bear markets. I was no kid, and I had been around the block a couple of times in the corporate world. I had built up a decent book of business. But even the best brokers two and half years in were way below those numbers, and they'd let you know that not so subtly and too often.

Guy "the Knife" had earned his nickname quickly when he'd moved from New Jersey to take over the branch. It was hard to be more of a Jerseyer than he, and it was a stretch to imagine him ever fitting in around genteel Virginia. When I broke the news to him after describing all I'd seen on our one-week trip to the Caribbean, I got a shocking response: "Why don't you stay with the company and work from Saint Croix?" Very un-Knife like. I would like to think it was because I had become invaluable to the branch, but more likely, it was because I had mentioned I'd learned of a couple of hedge funds there and a certain major player in worldwide CDs who kept tax-motivated headquarters on Saint Croix. The Knife was thinking about money, as always. Apparently, lending large sums to hedge funds and getting the margin account of the CD king via me could have made "the Knife" famous at Citigroup.

The entire idea of leaving our comfortable life in Alexandria was being made possible, and perhaps even wise, by the 2005–2006 real estate frenzy that was underway. Houses that had sold in the low three hundreds were getting bid up to twice that and sometimes almost a million. I talked constantly about how people in our area were spending "stupid money." They had it and were spending it frantically. Even the Vietnamese gal who cut my hair was flipping houses with no-doc loans three at a time, blind to the fact that in the end, she'd be holding the bag when it all hit the fan.

We had participated in the bubble and could be thankful for that, but I was convinced that it didn't have legs for much longer. So, with a commitment made on the Pink Fancy, our home of fourteen years, where the girls had grown up, went up for sale at $850,000. This was the highest price our Westgrove neighborhood had seen. But if we were to avoid tapping the retirement funds, we were still a half million short.

I had connections with former Texas Instruments executives, and a super trustworthy friend and former boss came to mind whom we could approach about privately financing the balance. Hank had been known to take some risks. He had always made good on his word and reputation—to the point of reimbursing several of us when a business he had suggested we loan money to turned out to have been run more like a Ponzi scheme by one of those shiny-faced Texas Christians. Hank had been lied to as a board member of that company, and we'd taken him at his word that the business was legitimate and our money safe. That lie to him could have cost several of us dearly. I had put in a huge chunk of my severance payout from TRW. A promised 15 percent dividend is hard to pass up when your salaried days are over.

When the shit hit the fan, Hank called all of the investors he had brought into the company and insisted on buying us out at our full investments. There was no obligation on his part to do this, but it showed what kind of guy he was. We had no idea what it all cost him, but he paid it, and the shiny-faced, Jesus-loving Christian went to jail. Lesson learned: 15 percent returns on no-risk loans or investments do not exist, even if the story sounds logical and the owner has fourteen photos behind his desk of his lovely family on the church steps.

So, the man who'd bailed us out before agreed to provide private financing for the Pink Fancy. Hank was a friend who solved the issue of our being $450,000 short of cash at closing. We would not fail him. This would be easy! Maybe we should have known better, but it did seem very doable.

The sixth task, starting to market the hotel even before we had officially closed on it, proved a challenge.

The sellers had been rather lax when it came to keeping records. We began to suspect that this was standard procedure for tax avoiders living an ocean away from IRS headquarters. But you'd think they'd cough up the real records when buyers asked. This was our first clue that these women were not being fully transparent—and also our first realization that we'd approached the deal like buying a residence, not a business.

Note to folks who are thinking of something like this...do not do what we did.

What do you mean, there is no customer list?

CHAPTER 11

Do We Have Partners? (Cal)

AFTER WE GOT the financing arranged, the deal looked good. Everything was falling into place. When our house sold, we wouldn't have to dip into our cash reserves or any of our retirement money. Could it actually get any better?

It was at about this time that a call came out of the blue from Joan's college roommate, Debbie. She and her husband wanted in on the deal. The whole adventure had, after all, been cued up by Joan's wine-aided phone call with Debbie close to eight months ago.

Debbie and Mike (who had been my best friend during our days at Bradley University) lived on the outskirts of Santa Barbara. They were both former educators and high-energy people. Mike was an entrepreneurial kind of guy, having run several cash businesses on the side—a driving range, a series of vending-machine franchises, and a car wash. They were now in the process of retiring and had sold most of those endeavors. They had done well and apparently accumulated some serious cash along the way.

We had a good relationship with these longtime friends in California. Joan and Debbie were as close as you can be when you are quite a distance apart. Their at-least-monthly calls were highlights of their motherhood experiences as they each raised two girls of similar ages. Mike and I loved to debate sports and politics, and we had been into jabbing at each other over them in nearly daily e-mails.

Was this a smart idea—doing business with lifelong friends? Usually, that's a sure way to get into a pissing contest and ruin a relationship. On the other hand, they were offering to be minority partners at 25–40 percent and relieve us on the island a month or two a year. That was a nice thought—vacation from a vacation—plus, maybe we could enter this venture with zero debt. It would be hard to fail…wouldn't it?

While I was wary, I was also quite intrigued. I wasn't, however, willing to take any step with them unless they saw the property, we did an appraisal (which I had not planned to do), and all four of us talked it through.

I saw being debt free as something well worth considering, though, so I put aside my concern about doing business with close friends and agreed to the partnership. We quickly put together a trip for us all. At least it would give us a second chance to really look things over before we actually closed on the deal.

The trip was a good idea.

CHAPTER 12

—— ❧ ——

The Second Trip (Cal)

JUMPING INTO MY tour-master mode, I made arrangements for the West Coast potential partners to fly into DC the following Thursday, and then we'd all fly to Saint Croix for a three-day fact-finding mission Friday morning. The Californians were serious about being in on the venture and were bringing a suitcase of cash—literally.

All went well, it seemed. The property was as we described, the current owners were as big a pain in the ass as we had warned, and, at least on this trip, the island showed well. On Saturday afternoon, after we'd all inspected the Pink Fancy and driven around the island to the point of exhaustion, we headed to the boardwalk for cocktails and a late lunch. There, we ran into Alaska Sam.

Sam had taken Joan and me on a kayaking expedition on our trip three weeks earlier. An impressive guy and certified free spirit, he trained sled dogs in the summer at his cabin way up north in Alaska, beyond the reach of civilization. He had done everything imaginable by the age of thirty-two. He'd been a cook on an Alaska crab boat, hiked the Appalachian Trail, and was a very competitive triathlete, damn good-looking, and an over-all smart and good guy.

We invited him to join us at Rum Runners, the open-air bar and restaurant we'd learned of on our first visit. He charmed Joan and Debbie over the fish tacos we'd offered to split with him after he'd guided the day's sail to Buck Island. Rum punches in hand, the college friends and their husbands excitedly told Sam of their plans to be hoteliers here in paradise. If the gals needed any confidence, Alaska Sam was ready to give it: "You can do this; you'll be great."

Hearing that expert opinion, we all decided to bring him by the fortress that was the Pink Fancy. He knew of it but, like many others on the island, had never been inside the gates. Along with him came his very nice and very pretty girlfriend, Jenny.

Jenny had come to the island, as many do, just to chill out after college. She'd found work on the day-trip boats to Buck Island. Sam had found her, and they were a thing. It became obvious to us that Jenny had longer-term plans for this exciting and handsome guy. He was sincere, but no woman could divert Alaska Sam from his chosen lifestyle.

Alaska Sam loved what he saw at the Pink. It may have been he who first told us, "All you have to do is..." It became a recurrent bit of advice we'd get from those with no skin in the game.

We showed Debbie and Mike as much of the island as time allowed, with much assistance from Mary. She took us on a great tour, and we stopped at an art show taking place at the botanical gardens. She introduced us to many of the artists and spectators there. When we were introduced to anyone as the new owners of the Pink Fancy, we heard the oddest comments. It seemed that the gals who had been running it were not very well liked, so everyone was thrilled that we were buying the place.

While we were at the art show, Joan found a painting of the Pink Fancy by a local artist and bought it as a surprise for me. It was actually of the cottage where we were presently staying. Mary agreed to keep it until closing so Joan could present it then as a housewarming gift. We were really getting into this whole idea more and more each day.

The owners had put us four in the two-room cottage up the hill, which worked out nicely, as we could talk away from other guests and the hovering sellers, who would have loved to hear what we were saying about their property.

We enjoyed showing Mike and Debbie all around the property—the parts we were allowed to go into, that is. High season was basically over, so there were only a few guests. Our partners seemed to like the rooms they saw, but once again, it seemed impossible to get in to see the schoolhouse building. The owners had put their feet down. Joan did convince them to let us take a quick peek at what would soon become our home. Once again, it didn't occur to us that we had every right to demand a thorough personal inspection of what we were buying.

Spike could be quite severe and abrupt and was fairly adept at browbeating people into submission. Here we were, buying the place—and not only were we paying full price right now for the rooms in which we were staying on this fact-finding trip, but we were actually being charged for every bottle of water we drank.

I suggested that Debbie, Mike, and I meet with Dora to discuss certain details while Joan met with Spike to go over how the office was run. I made this suggestion for expediency (and to get Spike out of the equation), as we had a lot to cram into four days. Apparently, this idea was not received well and drove Spike to tears and a tantrum. Dora came to our room and explained that Spike felt as though she was being left out. I explained my reasons for suggesting the scenario but said we were fine with it if we all met together.

After Dora left, Debbie made the comment that "Dora's wife is a bitch," which was basically true. After this incident, Spike relented and actually invited Joan into the kitchen, so she could finally see what kind of storage she would have. It wasn't much, to say the least, but Joan felt she could work with it and was happy that she had finally gotten to see what we were buying. What were we thinking?

The visit with Debbie and Mike did throw up some red flags. We felt that their experience as business owners would be helpful, and the idea that we could get off the island occasionally was comforting. But they all say that doing business with close friends can be a problem.

CHAPTER 13

The Appraisal (Cal)

THE TRIO OF Joan, Debbie, and Mike returned to the mainland on Monday. I stayed an extra day to visit with the appraiser, Mr. Collins, who had thrown some serious cold water on our deal.

He was doing his job, but I had specifically asked for a market-value and a replacement-value appraisal only, not a valuation as a business. Mr. Collins had done his appraisal all three ways and revealed the more complete results to all four of the prospective partners in a meeting arranged in our room at the Pink Fancy.

The room was called "Hard Labour," because, like all the rooms, it had been cutely named for one of the seventy-six sugar plantations that had given Saint Croix its first boom in the slavery years before 1840. It should have been an omen.

It is likely not easy to get a list of current comparable sales on an island in the middle of the Caribbean, especially for a historic property being used as a fourteen-room hotel with dubious financial records that the owners wouldn't reveal. In the absence of the financial records, Mr. Collins had used the reported island-wide occupancy rate of 28 percent to determine the expected cash flow of the business. The replacement value he arrived at exceeded the $1,195,000 price we had signed a contract to pay, but the business value was put at $650,000.

The line Mr. Collins used to sum it up haunted those in the room: "So, looking at this factually, if the hotel were destroyed by fire or in a hurricane, it would not make financial sense to rebuild."

After the appraiser left, Debbie and Joan collapsed on the king-size bed. We were not happy with the results. I explained to the rest of the team that I had asked the appraiser not to do the business appraisal because I knew that in the absence of accounting records, this would be the result. I was absolutely convinced that the owners' bottom line was far higher than what was on the books. I was sure that they did a healthy under-the-table cash business. I don't think the rest of the team were quite as convinced.

That night, I put pen to paper and tried to persuade myself. The contract was contingent on, among other things, the inspection and the appraisal; Joan felt that we could offer them what it had appraised for as a business, and they could either take it, or the deal would be null and void.

How could a 28 percent occupancy rate be accurate? My ever-optimistic mind did not want to hear that. After all, "all you had to do" was promote the place.

I was, if nothing else, a promoter.

CHAPTER 14

We Are on Our Own Again (Cal)

THE BUSINESS-OWNER VETERANS from the West Coast apparently better recognized the red flags. While I attended one of my last board meetings at Mount Vernon Country Club on the Wednesday evening after getting back from our trip, Joan fielded a call from her close friend, Debbie. She and Mike were out!

We hadn't seen this coming, and it was a setback. I had already informed Hank that we wouldn't be needing his private-investment loan, and I'd spread the word among friends at the club and at work that we'd found an unsolicited partner. After a few moments of "What the fuck?" it seemed we slept better that night knowing we hadn't poisoned a friendship with a business deal.

An April trip to California to visit daughter Sarah at UCLA provided the opportunity to return the suitcase of cash that our friends had intended as their investment. It is fairly exciting to board a plane with $68,500 in unmarked bills. You feel a bit like a courier in a suspense novel—especially when the rendezvous point is the Santa Anita Park racetrack.

While waiting outside the Turf Club for Mike to arrive, I couldn't help but show the contents in the briefcase to a longtime friend and mentor from Dallas who had come out as part of a gang I had organized for the running of the 2006 Santa Anita Derby, which happened to be that Saturday. Dan's eyes bulged as if he had found himself in the middle of a drug deal. My explanation sounded logical, and now Dan had a story to tell back at his retirement village.

Although it hadn't been discussed at the hand-off, I had removed $1,500, the amount I'd spent arranging the fact-finding trip for Debbie and Mike in March. I had volunteered to arrange and pay everything for the hasty trip with the thought that if they became partners, the expense would be a tax deduction for the Pink Fancy's LLC and passed on to us all, the owners, to offset all the planned profits.

Now that they'd withdrawn from the deal, it seemed logical to me that they should pay for their own trip, which had convinced them wisely not to do business with friends and perhaps woken them up to the fact that it was too radical an idea anyway, even if it had been theirs in the first place.

The day following the handoff at Santa Anita, I had the chance to explain the $1,500 I had removed. I asked Mike if he was OK with that. He said yes and nicely asked me if we were OK with them withdrawing. I confirmed that we were, and all seemed behind us regarding this close call with best-friend partnerships.

It was during the California trip when it hit that we were really all in. We received a call from our real estate broker who had listed our Alexandria home just the previous week: we had a "clean," full-price offer on it—$850,000, no conditions. We had no reason not to accept, so we did. Guess what, folks? We were officially committed.

We had a lot to do now, and there was no turning back. I was feeling like quite the operator, having brought twenty friends from all over to watch the ninety-fifth running of the Santa Anita Derby and the first and only running of the Pink Fancy Handicap at the track—race three of an eleven-race card.

It had been a fun day, and my ego was running high. If I could pull all *this* off, I could fill fourteen rooms in a classic Caribbean hotel in paradise.

CHAPTER 15

—— ❧ ——

The Move (Joan)

IN THE COURSE of our thirty-plus-year marriage, we had moved seven times. (We're now up to nine.) Moving is always exciting and, of course, has its share of stress. In this regard, this move wasn't that much different from the others. But it was also so much more. We were moving from a thirty-five-hundred-square-foot house into about eight hundred square feet of living space. To say we were downsizing didn't even begin to cover it. Although our daughters no longer lived with us, most of their stuff still did. So we had to sort through fourteen years of our own accumulation, and they basically had to sort through their entire lives. We had piles to throw away, give away, sell in a garage sale, and take with us. We assured the girls that we would store whatever they wanted for as long as necessary, as we were certainly causing upheaval in their lives, and they both had extremely small apartments.

In the end, we had to rent a ten-by-ten-foot storage space in Front Royal, Virginia, a small town at the base of Shenandoah National Park and Skyline Drive, where storage facilities were more affordable than in Northern Virginia. We had three garage sales and made uncountable trips to deliver items to the local thrift store and the public library. We had to sort through our younger daughter's things via telephone, since she couldn't make the trip from UCLA to do it in person. And after all of that, I still felt that we had way too much stuff to take with us. Cal kept assuring me that we had fourteen rooms in which to spread out, but I was concentrating on the two little rooms where we would live.

During this time, as part of the contract signed by both buyers and sellers, the current owners were obligated to run the hotel and take future bookings, and it was also agreed that one of them would stay for a month after closing to help us learn the ropes. We later discovered that they had actually closed the place for the entire month of June, spending that time in Europe on their next adventure as hotel owners. When we took over, we had absolutely no bookings and had to start from scratch.

CHAPTER 16

Everything Is Easy (Joan)

THE EXCITEMENT WAS growing, and it was contagious. Our friends and neighbors, who probably thought we were crazy, joined in the excitement and said they envied our sense of adventure. As one friend put it, "Lots of people I know say they'd like to do something like this, but none of them actually do it!"

Cal heard about a Caribbean hotel-association conference in Miami. He felt we could learn a lot and meet some good contacts, so even though we hadn't actually closed our deal yet, we joined the association and booked our reservations. Wendy, our soon-to-be webmaster and friend, who was based on Saint Croix, recommended two consultants for us to meet at the conference. Since we were totally ignorant about our new undertaking, we agreed that this was a good idea.

We flew to Miami, went to the various seminars, met some wonderful people (including the consultants, Richard and Marie), and generally had a great experience. We were beginning to believe that Dora had been right on the mark: everything was easy!

And so, we plunged full-speed ahead. The packers and movers came and collected what we hadn't sold or put into storage. We felt we had downsized big-time, although I still felt we were taking more than we needed and more than we had space for. Cal just kept insisting that we had fourteen rooms to use.

CHAPTER 17

— ❧ —

Doing It All (Cal)

THINKING I COULD make this drastic change in our lives with no impact was beginning to come into focus as time ticked down toward closing day and our impending move.

My habit of rarely saying no to any potential fun activity had certainly worn on Joan and others close to me over the years. Joan coped by enjoying her alone time and only joining in my hyperactivity when it suited her. I had built up a series of commitments with friends over a lifetime as a "yesaholic." Annually since 2002, I had organized and hosted the "Cal Coolidge Invitational" in late June at the Homestead Resort in Hot Springs, Virginia. I could pile eight to twelve competitive golfers into our Owners Club second home. The golf in this group was serious, but the evenings were full of stories over massive steaks, baked potatoes, and pies all prepared by my loyal caddies and their wives. Bart and John in particular seemed to love this additional duty. We always included them in the discussions, which were often led by the air-force generals who were my friends after my years of working around senior leadership in and around the Pentagon.

Every early August, I would join a dozen senior managers and golf enthusiasts from my Texas Instruments days for five days and eight rounds of golf at Pinehurst. Between these two blow-outs, I had also been part of an annual amateur Ryder Cup Team for the last nine years. It was a motley group of Americans of various skill levels who annually played a fun-loving but competitive and cohesive group of Europeans. We on the USA team had been getting beat regularly, but I'd committed to be on the team in Portugal this year.

With our closing date on the hotel set for July 9, one would think I'd have weaseled out of these commitments. Not me.

Ignoring Joan's reasonable suggestions that it was time to give up one lifestyle for the next, I was busy constructing a schedule that did it all. It would be easy!

June 25–27: Attend the Caribbean Hotel Owner's convention in Miami.

June 29: Close on the sale of our Virginia home.

June 30: Leave for Portugal with my Ryder Cup pals.

July 6: Return to Washington, stay with friends near Dulles.

July 7: Fly to Saint Croix.

July 9: Go to closing on the Pink Fancy, and begin a ten-day transition and training with the former owners.

July 19: Return to Washington, and host the annual Cal Coolidge Invitational at the Homestead.

July 28: Joan returns to Saint Croix alone, and I head to Pinehurst to join Dallas buddies for the annual Pinehurst golf tournament.

August 1: Cal returns to DC, sells Joan's Lexus SUV in one day, and flies to Saint Croix to join Joan (who will have been running the hotel for a week by herself).

August 5: Bring in our newly hired consultants to structure pricing and our Internet strategy.

August 7: Daughter Melinda flies to Saint Croix to help us with start-up.

What could go wrong?

CHAPTER 18

— ❦ —

Abbie (Joan)

AN EMOTIONAL ISSUE that "Mr. Positive, Don't Worry" Cal had not solved was how we would get Abbie, our thirteen year-old Beagle-ish rescue dog, to join us on this move. It was nonnegotiable with me that she would be included in this uprooting of my life.

We had investigated the process and learned that airlines would not fly a dog in a crate on a day that would exceed eighty degrees. It was very unlikely that, traveling as we were in early July, they would accept Abbie on our flights. Even if we had a cool morning at our departure airport, what would we do if it was going to be over ninety degrees that day in Miami, where we needed to transfer flights? I could picture the crisis that would erupt if we saw Abbie's crate being unloaded on the tarmac with Cal and me already on board. I would have fought my way off that flight to save her.

This potential crisis was a topic over dinner with Alexandria and Mount Vernon friends John and Deb as the month of June wound down. John had been following our adventure closely since we'd broken the news. He was the first of several to say, "People insist that someday, they are going to chuck it all in and move to the Caribbean. You guys are the only ones who are really doing it!"

As a free spirit, musician of sorts, and, at times, an overstressed defense executive in Washington, John envied our adventure in a way. It seemed that he and Deb had ever-shifting plans to escape the rat race, but they also loved the good life that their careers provided. Maybe someday! They did come to our rescue that evening, however. "We can take Abbie for a few months," John volunteered. "When it cools off in the fall, we can fly down with her. We want to see the hotel. It will be fun!"

Deb must have consented to this idea earlier, as she added, "This will give us a chance to see if we can handle a dog. We've talked about getting one, but we worry about our work schedules. Abbie is pretty low maintenance, isn't she?"

Wow. Cal and I looked at each other. We couldn't have been happier! Abbie, approaching fourteen, wouldn't feel abandoned. We'd get her to the island. It might be four or five months, but we'd have her back. I was thrilled.

Cal had dodged another bullet. The unsolvable issue had been solved. Thank you, John and Deb.

CHAPTER 19

Departure Day and the Emotions (Joan)

THERE WERE A few tears as we walked out of our Alexandria, Virginia home of fourteen years for the last time. The closing had gone flawlessly, though, and the Portugal trip was a fabulous opportunity for Cal and me to relax and work up the courage for what was to come.

We were riding high on the cool summer air of the Algarve region overlooking the Mediterranean. We commented many times that there was something different about this clean air that sweeps across the Atlantic that hadn't been touched by anything manmade for close to three thousand miles. I started to convince myself that Saint Croix would have this same crisp air. After all, "there is always a breeze."

Both the Americans and Europeans on the trip assured us they would certainly be traveling to see the Pink Fancy and, of course, to visit us. We were starting to think it would all be easy. After all, "all you had to do" was...

We'd asked Vade and Janet, former neighbors from the mideighties in Reston, if they could put us up upon our return near Dulles Airport. Just one night. When we had lived in Reston for three years, Janet and I had raised our kids together. This time, it was a great pleasure to relax with them on their shaded deck, drinking our share of wine, retelling stories of the kids' antics together, and fielding questions about this new adventure we were embarking on. Vade may have been skeptical.

It happened to be unusually cool on July 7, and Cal thought that maybe he should go get Abbie and risk putting her on the flight the next day. I vetoed that idea, but we did call John and Deb to check on our pup. They said that Abbie seemed to be doing fine. Visiting nephews and nieces were giving her plenty of love and enjoying her company. They confessed that she had given them a reason to leave work at a normal hour for the first time. "I need to let the dog out" is always an acceptable excuse to leave a meeting that should have ended hours ago.

I was relieved, my guilt subsiding for the moment.

Fancy That

Joan and Cal
have flown the coop.
Leaving behind
the beltway loop

A disappearing act
a la Siegfried and Roy,
leaving Foggy Bottom
for sunny St. Croix.

A little known fact
for what it's worth,
St. Croix is shorter
than the beltway's girth.

From puts and calls
and library books,
to guided tours
around bayou nooks.

The emphasis now
is on customer howls
for breakfast coffee,
fresh linens and towels

Is it a new life start
that we conservatives think chancy?
Or is it just something
that strikes their Pink Fancy

SDH August 2006

PART 2

We Own a Hotel

———— ✿ ————

CHAPTER 20

Arrival (Cal and Joan)

"WELCOME HOME," I whispered to Cal as our flight touched down in Saint Croix.

He squeezed my hand, "I'm a little scared, but this is going to be great," he said. I believed him.

We knew what to expect on the cab ride to the hotel. We'd get used to driving in the left lane, I was sure, but I had decided that Cal would doing the driving once we bought a vehicle and began further exploring the island.

Somehow, as actual residents now, we noticed certain things more. As we pulled up to the Pink Fancy on Prince Street to unload, we did not need to be terribly observant to note that the open field that had been vacant except for six to eight rental cars and a small tent that had apparently served as an office was now—oh my God—taken up by a forty-foot single-wide mobile home. It may have seemed like the perfect world headquarters for our rental-car entrepreneur neighbor, but he'd not thought out delivery or setup very well.

What he hadn't considered was that the lot had the topography of the Big Valley. High in the front along Prince Street, it was six to eight feet lower in the middle and sloping up to street level toward the back. He had likely planned to settle the forty-foot monstrosity in the low part of the valley that ran parallel to the street, and it might have looked OK there.

The delivery of this item had most assuredly not been by professionals. The far end had made it to the rise at the back of the lot, but the near end had become hung up along Prince Street not twenty-five feet from the entrance of our Pink Fancy. We looked at the not-very-attractive single-wide mobile home stretching diagonally across the vacant lot…with its only door about seven feet above the lot's lowest point.

The owner had positioned a yellow, six-foot stepladder on the ground to allow himself and presumably rental-car clients to climb up to the door. The entire mobile home sagged in the middle—down to about the fourth step of the makeshift stairway. Both ends were on high ground. This…thing…was a beautiful sight for our arriving guests to marvel over. Nothing short of a heavy-duty crane was going to resolve this mess.

Welcome to island life, Cal and Joan.

CHAPTER 21

❧

Our New Home
(Cal and Joan)

DORA WAS MOVING into one of the hotel rooms so we could have the owner's space. Spike, to just about everyone's delight, was already in Austria, running their new business. The plan was that we would close on the property on July 9, but Dora would continue to run it for a bit, as we had our previous travel commitments back home and would enjoy one last week of the good life at our Owner's Club home at the Homestead in Hot Springs, Virginia. Once we returned, Dora would train us before she left for good.

Dora's idea of training might have been a little different from what we needed and expected. Yet, she truly did preface every remark and instruction with the phrase, "It's easy." It reminded us of the comment we all get when we ask a young person how the heck to run the new computer you just purchased: "Oh, that's easy." When you are fifty-five and grew up before the Internet, don't you want to punch the kid?

For instance, I had asked Dora back in April about watering the numerous plants, flowers, and palms in the various gardens and on the patio. She had told me it was easy. This was, after all, the tropics, and she basically never had to water any of them. I wondered at the time how this could be true, especially since some were under overhangs and couldn't possibly get rain. Now, in July, I was hearing a different story from her...although it was still *easy*.

The hotel had three water cisterns, one solar water heater, and one regular water heater—and, of course, the swimming pool. Dora said that all she did to treat the cisterns was to add chlorine in the form of Clorox bleach to one of them; the other two had algae-eating fish, and that was all it took—easy. I told her I had read about periodically having to treat the walls of the cisterns, but she insisted that it wasn't necessary. Besides, these cisterns had "never" run dry, so the walls couldn't be treated.

The main building used the regular water heater, but our building, the cottage, and the kitchen used the other, solar-powered heater. What a huge energy saver this would be (more on that later).

The pool was beautiful. It was all tile, and the water was as clear as any I've ever seen. This also, explained Dora, was so easy to maintain. Again, all she did was add chlorine (that is, Clorox bleach) as needed. Nothing else. We'd never had a pool before, but I knew most people did more than this to maintain them. I supposed that some things *were* easier in the tropics. Dora showed Cal the pool pump, and they had a lesson in backwashing it.

I didn't partake in this once I heard that if you screw it up, there could be an explosion. At that point, Cal was definitely beginning to feel out of his element and slightly stressed about the whole undertaking.

Even the phone system was stressing us out—not that it was ringing all that much. We had very few bookings, but this, of course, would certainly change as high season approached and the weather on the mainland worsened, making people want to escape to paradise. Yes, high season would change everything, if only we could figure out the phone system.

As our first day of training came to an end, I was taking everything in stride, one new thing at a time. At five thirty, I was ready to sit down and enjoy our first Pink Fancy punch, a recipe we had developed with some Internet help (and before we discovered the cost of juices on the island). The phone rang for the first time that day, and Cal answered, ready to book visitor number one. "Pink Fancy Hotel; this is Cal. Can I help you?" He would be a natural, you'd think. He apparently knew the caller, as the conversation became familiar, and he started his normal banter with some old friend who, I assumed, had tracked us down to wish us well.

Suddenly, Cal was quiet—no more jovial laughter. "Really," I heard him say softly. "When did this happen?" He was entirely serious all of a sudden. Cal walked out of earshot to the side of the pool as the conversation continued. His back was to me standing in my one-butt kitchen. I tried to get on with mixing our drinks.

When Cal turned back toward me after hanging up the phone, he was pale. He came over to me, obviously shaken. "Abbie died this morning."

I collapsed to my knees and then ran into our bedroom to be alone and weep. I had abandoned her, and she had died. *I am a terrible mother.*

We were alone. Cal hugged me, also crying softly. We felt devastated. When we finally got it together, Cal finished making our new punch concoction and coaxed me out to our deserted pool. At that very moment, the first of many rainbows that bless Saint Croix often in the late afternoons vividly broke into view. We cried some more. Abbie was looking down on us, alive, but the rainbow somehow was saying good-bye. She had loved being our dog, and we had loved her so much.

The Pink Fancy Punch Recipe

Equal parts, Guava Juice and Pinapple Juice. 1/4 part Orange Juice

Large quantities of Cruzan Rum –Mango Flavor preferred.

A wedge of Lime or an Orange for decoration.

(Make in mass quantities for best results)

CHAPTER 22

Training (Joan)

To say that we were becoming more overwhelmed on a daily basis is not an exaggeration. The previous owners, we were learning, were, shall I say, frugal with their money, perhaps out of necessity. Although the hotel was cosmetically beautiful, we were beginning to have our doubts about the condition of the infrastructure. The phone system was hardly state of the art, and in order for us to receive a fax, some fancy footwork was necessary (involving running from one room to another). Cal was stymied by the pool-pump system, the cistern system, and water-heating contraption, not to mention the electrical system and fuse box, which was a tangle of wires going absolutely everywhere and nowhere simultaneously none of which were labelled of course. In October our new found electrician friend Andre and Cal would spend an entire weekend on our walkie-talkies shutting off a circuit breaker and scurrying from one room to another to see which lights and outlets were affected.

Then the fire marshal came to inspect the property. Dora was still there, so, of course, this would be easy. I stayed out of the way, with a peek every now and then to eavesdrop. It really didn't go too badly, but don't try telling Cal that. He expected the marshal would come, look, pass us, and leave. We were told we needed to have all of the fire extinguishers checked and, if necessary, replaced (there was one in every guest room, of course). We needed to put escape-route plan signs in every room; I don't know why they weren't there already. Dora remained silent on that subject. The gates, however, were major.

There were three gates: the guests entered through the front ones, and only we used the back one for disposal of garbage and unloading supplies. When guests checked in, they were given two keys: one to their room and one for the front gates, which were always locked. We were noticing, now that we lived here, that we were in a neighborhood that some might describe as "the hood." The back gate was padlocked at all times. When we got the report from the fire marshal, we were informed that for us to pass inspection, this would have to change. The locks on both would need to be changed so that guests did not need a key to leave the premises by either exit in case of fire. But if we changed the locks, there would be no security, as anyone could just reach through the bars and unlock them. Steel mesh would have to be added to prevent this.

As we realized what we would have to spend to pass the follow-up inspection, Dora was her usual easy self: "Just go to the hardware store, buy the locks, and install them yourselves. And buy the mesh, and so on. It's easy." Since Cal was not a locksmith nor a welder, services that would be required to attach the mesh were going to be expensive. Cal had expected to just breeze through the fire inspection. He became angrier with each additional dollar we spent.

Have I mentioned how hot it is in July and August in the tropics? Well, I should, and I will probably get repetitive on that subject. Up to now, Cal had been changing shirts several times by noon each day. Longtime residents assured us that we would soon be acclimated. Since "soon" is a relative term, we tried to pin them down on how long it might take us to get used to the heat. The answers varied from one to five years! More than one person claimed that in the winter months, they actually used flannel sheets! To this day, I find that hard to believe.

In the middle of all of this angst, our shipment of household goods was on its way, which was a good thing...sort of. It would be nice having some of our own furniture again. When delivery day arrived, it took all day to unload the crate, not because the guys doing it were slackers, but because there was so much stuff, and everything had to come through the locked gate and up the seventeen steps of stone. As we were directing placement, even Dora was awed by the amount of goods we had shipped to our new home, which was already mostly furnished. We filled up our two rooms and put some things in guest rooms. We took a lot of furniture and boxes to the attic, which, fortunately, was quite large. At the end of the day, we still had many boxes outside, under the overhangs. There were few guests to deal with, which could be construed as either good or bad.

We spent a good part of the next week unpacking boxes and trying to find places for everything. The kitchen had one drawer, and around the third day of unpacking, Cal, sweat streaming down his face, asked me why the silverware tray was still sitting on the counter. I patiently (not) explained that since I only had one drawer, I needed to unpack all of the kitchen boxes before deciding which items were the most logical ones to put in the drawer. Of course, in the end, it was the silverware tray. One morning when I awoke and stumbled to the kitchen to greet the dogs and get coffee, Cal looked at me and said how sorry he was, that I had been right, and that we had brought much more than we needed or could place.

The day arrived for Dora's departure. I had very mixed feelings about this. On the one hand, she had begun to annoy me. If I heard how easy everything was one more time, I would have been tempted to throttle her. On the other hand, Cal and I were both terrified to be left on our own. With everything we learned each day, ten more questions would arise. I had little faith that Dora would bother responding to any e-mail questions once she was gone, and I was right.

One little issue was raised with Dora the day before she left us. The shower that Cal was trying to use so I could have my own bathroom was not draining. Water from the previous day's shower still stood there, only about an inch lower than when Cal had stepped out into the terribly humid air that immediately put him back into the sweating mode he was becoming famous for. Dora, of course, said, "Oh, that only happens a couple of times a year. Something may be blocking that drainpipe, but it would cost five hundred dollars to get a plumber in here to dig it up. Just let it go down slowly, and maybe don't use it in July or August. That's when this has happened in the past."

They had saved the $500, I guess, but standing water in Cal's already steamy shower and bathroom wasn't going to sit well. The problem did get solved a couple of months later. The cause of the blockage was not seasonal. A small lockbox was inexplicably blocking a strange dry sink below the bathtub drain.

So now, we were truly on our own and would have to deal with whatever problems arose with no assistance. The major one was a lack of bookings, present or future. There would be very little money coming in and apparently plenty going out. Take, for instance, electricity. On the mainland, electricity costs most people about seven cents a kilowatt-hour. On Saint Croix, it's forty-nine cents. Yes. Think about the bill you get monthly, multiply it by seven, and then remember that this was a fourteen-room hotel with air conditioners and a pool. We nearly fell over when the first bill arrived.

After Dora's departure, we would have a little more help, as we had hired the consultants that we had met at the Miami conference. They arrived three days after Dora's departure. At the same time, Melinda would arrive for her first visit to her parents' new home. So we did have those things to look forward to.

The consultants, Richard and Marie, were very nice and charming and really were a huge help. In fact, in the end, both Melinda and Cal agreed that hiring them was money well spent. But it was still more money going out than coming in. Cal wasn't always thrilled with all their suggestions, because, of course, almost everything they suggested would cost money.

The consultants stayed for five days. We weren't serving breakfast at this point. The previous owners had only served breakfast during high season. We had intended to serve it year-round, but we decided not to start until November. We felt we had enough to deal with without serving breakfast to our very few guests. We were obligated, however, to feed Richard and Marie three meals a day, which was an additional expense. And we gave them two of our best rooms. At least this was no hardship, since people weren't exactly banging down our gates to get them.

So, each day, we found new ways to spend. Richard and Marie took us through all the rooms. We were definitely going to have to replace all linens, eventually. Many of the sheets were stained, and the towels were adequate but needed to be upgraded. It was odd, all of the things we hadn't noticed before. Dora had told me that the guests were staining the sheets and to expect it, but when I did eventually replace the queen-size linens, I realized that the staining was coming from either the washer or dryer—so as soon as I washed my immaculate new sheets, they had stains on them. The washer and dryer were down the back stairs and basically open to the elements.

So, on top of replacing all of the linens, we would need to replace the washer and dryer at some point. Richard and Marie also said that we would need to eventually replace the bedspreads and, over time, the mattresses. This all certainly sounded overwhelming at first, but we decided we would wait to get through our first high season so we would have more money—hopefully.

One simple suggestion they made really rubbed Cal the wrong way. In each room, there was a collection of books. They said we had to get rid of all of them; apparently guests have been known to complain on Trip Advisor that books that offended them had been placed in their rooms specifically to target their beliefs. Seems weird to me. Marie said we could keep them in the bookcase on the patio. When we had first stayed there as guests, we'd thought the books in our room were a nice touch. So, one of the things we did bring with us was a large part of our book collection. Now we were being told we shouldn't put our books in the rooms. I'm not sure why Cal took such umbrage at this, but he did. Melinda had to sneak into each room and take out the books when he wasn't looking. She also cleaned all the ceiling fans and the bathroom exhaust vents. The ceiling fans looked as if they'd never been cleaned, and the bathroom vents were moldy. There was mold on some of the shower curtains, too. I have no idea why we hadn't noticed any of this on either of our two whole visits to inspect the place. Obviously, we saw only what we wanted to see.

Richard and Marie helped us to restructure a complicated pricing system so that we charged for only two types of rooms: deluxe and value. This sounded simple and logical, but what we later learned is that everyone wants a bargain. Even though our prices were reasonable and in line with other inns in the area, nearly 100 percent of people who called tried to get a lower price. I have never called a hotel to book a room and attempt to get a lower price. It just never occurred to me. But almost without exception, callers asked for a discount. And since we were desperate for business, we usually cut deals with them. At one point, we ran an introductory special for sixty-nine dollars, discounted from about one hundred—and, sure enough, people wanted it for thirty-nine. Cal eventually got so disgusted that he asked one caller how much we should pay *him* to stay at our hotel. I don't think that caller booked a room.

Richard and Marie helped Wendy, our webmaster, to update the hotel website with the new pricing, new links to island activities, and a picture of us (this latter being truly awful). The booking system we had inherited was as antiquated as anything I'd ever seen. Basically, it was a notebook with a piece of graph paper for each month, with the rooms crossed out when they were booked. The consultants insisted that we needed online booking. Currently, the only way people could find the hotel was on its own website, and they could only make reservations by calling directly. I learned that Cal had found it by Googling "hotels for sale." Not good. So they set us up with a system bookable through the big online systems such as Expedia and Travelocity. Of course, all of this came at a price, with little money coming in as yet. Plus, I had to be trained to manage all of the reservations and try not to overbook...though there seemed little chance of that happening.

CHAPTER 23

꯸

The Clorox Solution (Cal)

THE THOUGHT OF pouring Clorox into the water that our
guests would be drinking was not comforting to cistern
virgins such as ourselves. We didn't want to complicate
the process, but I found it worthwhile to inquire about it
at the Gallows Hardware store, where I was fast becoming one of their best clients—to the tune of about $1,000
every week, as daily I would encounter something that
had looked cosmetically wonderful, only to touch it or
turn it on and have it fall off the wall or go up in smoke.

Water-purification systems were available, but I
learned that as long as you were treating more than ten
thousand gallons, the Clorox solution was widely used
on the island. Chemicals such as fluoride were also suggested. Testing of the cistern water showed its chemical
balance to be acceptable. I wouldn't say that cistern water
had a perfect taste, but it was the practice on any island
without a fresh water supply, and it was safe.

A stop by the pool-supply store yielded a different
opinion of the Clorox-only policy. Admittedly, the pool
was clear as a bell, but I had noted that several of the
two-inch square tiles were missing, and a few others had

come loose as I took daily dips at the end of my early cleaning shifts. Bobby, the apparent owner of Sunny Isle Pool and Spa Services, encouraged me to bring in a water sample. He, of course, sold chemicals—and I was about to become a $300-per-month customer.

My trip back to the pool service with a jug of clear water was uneventful. In hindsight, I was lucky that the water didn't eat a hole in the bottom of the old peanut-butter jar I used.

Bobby poured the nice, clear water into his testing device. He commented, as he caught a whiff, "Might be a little high on alkalinity." He explained, "Pure water would show about one to three parts per million of chlorine. Chlorine is quite effective at eliminating bacteria and mold at those levels, but when it gets much higher, it needs to be balanced with acid to keep the alkalinity down."

The testing machine started flashing a two-digit number that I could just make out across the counter: 10.2...10.2...10.2.

Bobby stopped the lecture on chemistry suddenly. "Is anyone using this pool?"

I answered that I had dived in daily for the past week, but no guests had been in since we'd taken over. "If you are in this more than five minutes, your hair should be turning green within a week. Is there any grout in this pool?"

"Do you mean between the tiles?" I responded.

"Trust me," said Bobby. "If this pool has been sitting at these levels for any amount of time, the grout will be gone. I need to come see what you are dealing with. I am coming over on my way home. In the meantime, rope it off. Pure Clorox registers at thirteen point oh."

Thus began the $4,300 process of draining, regrouting, and purchasing a tanker or two full of desalinated water to return the oldest pool in the Caribbean to a usable and marketable feature of the Pink Fancy Hotel. I had violated my lifelong philosophy regarding pools: "If you want a swimming pool, join a country club that has one!"

CHAPTER 24

— ✺ —

History Revisited (Cal)

IT WAS EXCITING, if increasingly expensive, to own a historic property, even though we found that the locals took it all for granted. We never did break into the rumored Saint Croix Landmarks Society, if in fact it still existed. The closest we came was when we hosted a tour for the garden club, during which the well-heeled of the island eyed our grounds and made comments that pleased us—such as, "I never knew this was so beautiful"—and some that troubled us—like, "Why haven't we ever been allowed in here before?" We were finding out how isolated the previous owners had chosen to be from the local business and inherited-wealth communities.

It was never clear to us when that romantic notion of a writers' haven owned by a former dancer in the Ziegfeld Follies had become the labor of love and later despair for the next known celebrity to pour his heart, not to mention a fortune, into.

We only heard vague stories about the Pink Fancy's history from the 1960s. We had one faded, black-and-white photo of that era found in a file that showed a bar set up about where the ice machine now sat at the far end of the pool. We heard rumors that at one time, the pool had been covered up with a dance floor.

Guests enjoying the poolside bar, circa 1960s

In the 1960s and early '70s, Saint Croix was the place to be. In fact, the Caribbean welcomed celebrities and interesting characters that it seems our modern age produces fewer of. It was in about 1971 that Sam Dillon, who was born in 1912, heir to apple orchards in western Maryland and previously an owner of a hotel in Hagerstown, Maryland, took the plunge and bought the Pink Fancy. It was said that he did this with the encouragement of Mary Pomeroy, a rather eccentric woman who spent time on Saint Croix along with her close friend Maureen O'Hara, a movie star, and her celebrity husband, World War II Brigadier General Charles Blair, who were living on the island. General Blair had once been the senior pilot for Pan Am airlines, and he was the founder of the US Virgin Islands airline Antilles Air Boats. Maureen O'Hara had starred in a string of movies in the 1940s, '50s, and '60s opposite nearly every leading man in Hollywood, but most often John Wayne.

Mary Pomeroy, who would later disappear—much like Amelia Earhart—in 1990 while flying solo from Nevis to Saint Croix in her plane the *Broomstick*, was known to be a character you could not have dreamed up. She had been born in 1909 on Malta in the Mediterranean, her father one of the last Knights of Malta.

Much of Mary's past is as shrouded in mystery as her disappearance. Well-known for her eccentricities, strong opinions, and propensity to guard her properties with a shotgun, it was rumored that she might have been involved in gunrunning during the Spanish Civil War, been a spy for the British in Italy, and delivered planes from Antigua to Africa for the United States during World War II.

In the 1960s, Mary had turned a financially failing plantation on Nevis into a guesthouse called Nisbitt's Plantation for the rich and famous of Europe, but she later found herself kicked off Nevis for her constant criticism of the local government, a practice brought to a head by her dumping a pile of defamatory literature from the cockpit of her single-engine plane over the governor's mansion on Saint Kitts. In retaliation, her property was seized and put up for auction while she was away on one of her many adventures. She repeated the Caribbean hotel plan on Saint Maarten's, buying what would become Mary's Boon Beach Plantation in 1970.

Sam and his wife, Dorothy, might well have found in her stories the adventure they had been seeking in retirement. Sam, it was said, had lived a meaningful life. His career had included orchids, the Hagerstown hotel, and popularity that had landed him in the Maryland House of Delegates in the 1950s and '60s. Memories of Sam and Dorothy were alive on the island when we arrived in 2006, even though they had departed it in the mid-1980s—and life itself in the early 2000s. They had been a gracious couple who'd poured over a million dollars into the Pink Fancy.

In the barroom discussions I began to have with aging locals when we got away from the hotel for a cocktail or three, we learned that they had probably been the first of a series of "owners" to learn that the math just didn't work when it came to the finances of this Caribbean classic, the Pink Fancy.

We'd heard of the owners Nan and Wendell, who had survived Hurricane Hugo with a hotel full of petrified guests. They were followed by the late Big Jim and Mona, and then, of course, the "gals." What we hadn't heard was that there had never really been successive owners.

Two months after closing, when the deed of trust was finally delivered to us, I learned that no one had ever really relieved Sam and Dorothy of ownership. The paperwork I read through in private showed that the estate of Sam and Dorothy Dillon had held the mortgage for each of the successive owners. Very likely, each time an owner had thrown in the towel, Sam or Sam's estate (now based in California with his offspring) had negotiated a new and probably smaller note with the next in the parade.

After we paid just under $1.2 million cash, for the first time since the 1970s, the estate of Sam Dillon was out of the Caribbean hotel business. When I read the details of who had received $220,000 of that sum, a sinking feeling went through me. I had just learned how truly hard it was to sell a small hotel in Saint Croix. Damn near impossible! I did not share this with Joan.

CHAPTER 25

— ❧ —

All This Gets You Thinking (Cal)

WE NEVER DID receive a thank-you note from Sam's heirs.

This whole facing of reality started making me un-characteristically paranoid. I had time while cleaning toilets in the occasional guest's room to think about why Sam had come this far to spend a million-plus dollars to get into a business that apparently he had already been in up north. I came across correspondence with contractors showing he had abruptly shut down even more planned improvements in March 1973. One letter in an old file had come from a disappointed contractor who claimed he had incurred over $200,000 in purchase advances for a planned expansion into the two vacant lots alongside the existing hotel. He had demanded to know why Sam had cancelled the verbal contract they'd had, and he'd threatened legal action.

I once read that Maryland politics rivaled only those of Joan's home state of Illinois, which included a his-tory of missing funds as one of Illinois's governors was sentenced to ten years to life. Maryland's most famous case came to a head with Spiro Agnew's resignation as

Richard Nixon's vice-president. The thought crossed my mind that a delegate on the transportation committee, throughout an era of interstate-highway construction, might just know where a few million in state-issued securities might be best cashed, spent, or stored—likely not close to home.

Post Agnew's very public bribery case in 1973, cashing large quantities of Maryland transportation bonds would draw attention even fifteen hundred miles away.

All of this was only in my newly paranoid mind. I never heard a negative or suspicious word regarding Mr. Dillon on the island.

CHAPTER 26

The Guests (Joan)

WE DISCOVERED A strange phenomenon early on: inn-keepers don't get to choose their guests. They are just grateful to have them, for the most part. This was not to say that all our guests were strange or difficult; we had our share of wonderful, fun, and delightful ones.

There was Sue, who was with us for a month while looking for a place to live. She worked for the schools for a year, and she became one of my closest friends on the island. And there were shorter-term guests, like Zach, who were great to have.

Eddie and Susie came to get married on the beach. And we got to be their witnesses! I was so excited. It was just the four of us and Captain Ed, who performed the ceremony. It actually made me look forward to future guests and possibly future weddings. At the other end of the age spectrum were Jerry and Mildred, who had spent their honeymoon on the island at a different hotel called the Cloverleaf. They had come back for their fiftieth an-niversary and stayed with us. Cal had a great time taking them all around and had them interviewed for the local paper. He was able to locate the hotel they had stayed in originally by calling on our original tour guide, Sweeney, whose memory went back far enough to know of it. The Cloverleaf had closed in the early 1970s, and although it was now an overgrown ruin that one needed a machete to get to, they were able to "tour" it.

We practically adopted five pilots who were in training with the seaplane company. They were great guys and were happy to help us with chores like replacing ceiling fans. Eddie was actually part of this group, but he and Susie had been fortunate enough to find an apartment to rent on the property directly behind us. They became our "back-door guests." They knew we only locked the back gate at night, and they would let themselves in to visit and relax around the pool just like family, which they were.

These were people you would enjoy meeting and getting to know under any circumstances. These were people you would invite to your home and enjoy having as houseguests. Then there was the other side of the coin: people you definitely wouldn't want to get to know, let alone have as houseguests—even paying ones.

Mary Blake (rhymes with flake) spent a great deal of time on the phone from San Antonio with Cal, negotiating the price for her five-night stay. Cal finally relented, since we really needed the money a paying guest would provide, even though it was less than it should have been. Cal warned me before she even arrived that she would most likely be difficult. She was planning to move to the island and was there to check out the possibilities. A large percentage of the guests we had were either thinking of moving there or already had decided and were in the process.

Mary seemed nice enough when she checked in, and in all honesty, she was nice. But she was one of those people who know everything about everything. Everyone knows at least one person like this, but I'm talking extreme here. Twenty minutes after checking in, she informed us that she had taken the air conditioner in her room apart and cleaned the mold for us. She could tell immediately that it needed it. This was probably true, but as I've noted before, this is a constant battle on an island. She borrowed basically all of our pots and pans, so I had to scrounge for the other guests. She visited various businesses on the island to scout things out for her future and proceeded to tell the owners how to run them. She bragged one night that the only restaurants worth going to were those recommended by cab drivers, as they were the experts.

On her second night, she went to one with which we weren't familiar, and I made the mistake of asking her how she had liked it. It was so awful! Her salad had been swimming in oil, so she'd sent it back, along with everything else she'd ordered. She had also gone into the kitchen—she claimed—and told them everything they were doing wrong. Although there are many excellent restaurants on the island, I decided I would not recommend any to her for the duration of her visit, even though that was part of our job as concierges.

Cal Coolidge and Joan Coolidge

A young man called very late one evening and asked the price for a night, which he proceeded to negotiate. Cal, I hope he won't mind me saying, was desperate for paying guests at this point as well, and a deal was struck. Darren showed up with his very pregnant girlfriend. They seemed quite nice. In the middle of the next afternoon, Darren asked me to show him how to turn on the refrigerator in the room. Despite what they were paying, we had given them a deluxe room in the cottage, away from the main building. We quite often did this because most of the value rooms were down on the street level, and it was a real chore to haul all of the cleaning materials down the seventeen steps of stone.

So I followed him up to the cottage and into the room, where Jasmine was totally naked, uncovered on the bed. No one else seemed to think it odd that she hadn't put something on and maybe even gotten out of bed. I showed Darren how to control the fridge and quickly left.

He was paying cash, by the night, unless he was a little short, of course. As far as I could tell, he made his money by selling CDs and DVDs—pirated, maybe? I didn't want to know. The pregnant Jasmine apparently was about seven months along and felt compelled to get a lot of rest—like 24–7. This made it difficult to get into the room to clean, and when the next day's new arrivals took the room next door, they immediately came down to complain about the smoke smell. Smoking was strictly forbidden in all rooms. We warned Darren and Jasmine.

They denied it, of course, but it was definitely there. I believe they checked out soon after this—for the time being.

A few weeks later, the phone rang in the middle of the night. This happened fairly often, and it rarely had a good outcome. I almost always slept through it, but Cal is a light sleeper. I kept encouraging him to not answer the phone late at night, but he insisted that whatever business we could get was better than nothing.

When I got up the next morning, Cal told me that he had done something that was not going to make me happy. Darren had called from the front gate, and Cal had rented him a value room downstairs at street level. He was right: I wasn't happy. The still very pregnant Jasmine again never left the room. She also tried to cook something on the mini-kitchen burner using a dinner plate provided in the kitchenette. Although she didn't burn down the whole hotel, the room smelled like smoke again, and the plate was ruined. Apparently, she had also decided to open a beauty parlor in the room. By the time Cal got fed up enough to tell them to leave, we had to deal with the odor from the near-miss fire, cigarette burns in the bedding, and hair everywhere. For weeks, Cal found hair every time he vacuumed that room. When eventually one of our great pilot guests took the room, he had to ask for a broom, because there was still hair to be found.

There were other guests who stayed long-term while moving to the island. I guess like us, the idea of moving to a tropical island seemed romantic and adventurous and maybe even daring. But it seemed that at least some of these people—with the exception of us, of course—were at least slightly weird. It seemed to us that people who moved to Caribbean islands were often running from something.

There was Jackie, another one who had a better way to do everything, even though he was young and quite limited in life experiences. He also, like the famous Mary Blake, alienated business owners around us with his constant interference, to the point where they asked him to leave and not return. About three weeks into his month stay with us, he found a dead, mostly decayed rat in a flower pot about twenty feet from his room after weeks of complaining about an odor that none of us could pinpoint. Apparently, Peanut had found a new place to deposit her kills.

Ah, and then there was Paula, who was nice enough but did tend to spend her evenings at the breakfast table outside of the kitchen with her computer and several bottles of wine. She was known to help herself to my wine in the kitchen fridge when she ran out. Her stay just happened to coincide with that of the "mortifying mortician," as Cal dubbed her.

—— ❧ ——

CHAPTER 27

The Mortician (Cal)

PERHAPS OUR MOST disturbing guest was the one we named the "mortifying mortician."

Mr. Shanks, a slender, dignified islander, was highly respected. He owned and ran the premier funeral home on Saint Croix. When his father, Liam, died in the August after our arrival, we witnessed a tribute suited for a king.

Mr. Shanks Sr. had served the people of the USVI honorably as mayor of Christiansted, as the USVI's congressional representative, and as governor of the USVI—all with nary a whisper of the corruption that seemed to plague all other politicians on the islands.

The funeral attracted visitors to the island, including family members, political colleagues, and friends—they all would be coming. The word went out to hotel owners that all our rooms would be needed. This was welcome news to us struggling newbies. But our phone did not ring.

Although I felt a twinge of guilt, I called Mr. Shanks to express my condolences but, more importantly, to ensure that he was aware the Pink Fancy was available. He expressed appreciation, but the massive funeral with bands and bleachers for the overflow crowds went on with no grievers at the Pink Fancy.

Maybe my call of condolence at least made Mr. Shanks aware that we were anxious for business. Not more than three weeks passed before we answered a call from our new friend. Did we have room for a candidate he was bringing in from the States? She would be interviewing as a mortician; he was excited to have her coming. Would we ensure she had a nice experience?

A week's reservation at rack rate was important to us at this point. We set aside one of the best rooms, Upper Love, and had it fully prepared on Thursday, when we expected the mortician candidate. She was to arrive at about 11:00 a.m., which meant she was on the first of three daily flights from Miami.

No word had come by 1:00 p.m., when I finished the daily chores and had deleafed the pool for the fourth time. The afternoon passed slowly.

Joan was on her daily antimold campaign with the bucket, a coarse broom, and her trusty Clorox mix. She was determined to keep up with the black spots that magically appeared on our lovely Mexican tile surrounding the pool and on our lovely walkways to the four historic buildings that made up the compound of the Pink Fancy.

As cocktail time approached, I was antsy and needed to get off the property...but not too far. I needed to make sure the mortician's first impression was a good one.

A quick trip up Hamilton Street to the "KraZi Stans" was all I could afford; these boys' home was in earshot from the hotel, with only the fabulous home of Mona between. There was no telling what the boys would be up to. We had met them on one of our first days after Dora had departed. They were some of the funniest guys ever and provided comic relief for us during times when our own humor had left us.

The house of the "KraZi Stans" (their last names were Kramer and Zimmer; they shared the same first name of Stanley) was tight to Hamilton Street and very vertical. Like many stately homes in shouting distance of the harbor, the grounds had several small structures that provided a series of $600 rents to the owners (this was all that the cast of characters who made up the island's transient working poor could afford). The main living quarters were on the second floor, which overlooked the typically potholed Hamilton Street. The overgrown nature of the greenery and large mango trees thankfully blocked the view onto the "projects" that had been built as part of the Great Society, we supposed. They lay to the left. The Stans had arranged for a midnight removal of two larger trees that had blocked the narrow view of the beautifully blue Christiansted Harbor slightly to the right.

The boys also had devised a pulley system that I envied every time I hauled what seemed like tons of liquid up the seventeen steps of stone from street level to the hotel-reception area at the Pink. The KraZi Stans could position their pickup truck directly below the second- and third-floor porches of their home upon returning from shopping and hoist their groceries, booze, and massive quantities of the liquids we all consumed in the heat of Saint Croix's midsummer.

I found the KraZi Stans home after yelling through the iron gate outside the entrance to Lazy Sam's apartment on street level. This Sam was the self-proclaimed "laziest white man on the island." He had visited us at the Pink Fancy soon after we arrived, looking for work. The conversation had centered around the things he wouldn't do and the hours he couldn't work. He had narrowed down his interests to answering the phone—providing he didn't have to sit in our tiny office, that is. Poolside would be fine with him. And, "Could you get a larger umbrella?" Sam liked to follow the KraZi Stans to Styxx, an open-air bar on the boardwalk where the harbor's finest would gather. It didn't take a lot of energy. He remained happily unemployed.

My conversation with our fun neighbors the KraZi Stans hadn't yet reached the sitting-down-with-rum stage when some commotion erupted on Hamilton Street below. The sound of bags being dragged across the broken pavement and upstairs aroused my attention. Was Mona expecting guests? The KraZi Stans would have known that. But they were clueless. Could this be the wayward mortician?

I bounded down the gray stone steps, past the still-open door of Lazy Sam, and back out the iron gate. An SUV had its doors on both sides open on the narrow street. I heard knocking on the large colonial-era wooden doors and a native voice shouting, "Inside! Inside!" I had learned that "Inside!" is a logical thing to shout when that is where you prefer to be. It does take mainlanders a time to catch on. It is normal on Saint Croix.

Along with the native islander was a short, well-groomed man in his midsixties and a quite attractive woman in a short white skirt, sandals, and a well-pressed blouse that featured bright flowers. She impressed me as about thirty-five, and I would never have pegged her as a mortician. In what would be the last pleasant moment for eight days, I made my presence known, asking if I could help them.

"We are checking in to the hotel," responded the black man, whom I had to assume was the driver for this couple.

"The Pink Fancy?" I inquired.

The driver's memory must have been six or seven years old. Mona and her late husband, Big Jim, had "owned" the hotel for several years, or so legend had it. Perhaps they had used North Street as the entrance via their majestic historic home. If that was the case, I had not heard the story.

"Yes, the Pink Fancy...I am Reuben," the driver and cousin of Mr. Shanks identified himself, revealing a smile of perfect white teeth. Without asking for him to explain why he wasn't ringing the bell at the obvious entrance at 27 Prince Street around the corner, I trotted up the majestic circular stone staircase leading to Mona's front door, grabbed one of the four bags, and said, "Come with me. We'll use the back entrance."

Everyone seemed social, pleasant, and sober. I had never been good at recognizing a drunk.

———— ✂ ————

CHAPTER 28

Check-In (Cal)

WE WENT UP through the littered back entrance, past three garbage cans, the open-air laundry, and the vacant space where the portable generator should have been— if not for that ugly fire incident about sixteen seconds into our first attempt to start the machine a week after taking possession of the hotel.

The generator had had less than four hours of use on its timer but had the look of a neglected item when the change of ownership took place. Looking back, it is hard to recall the reassuring words Dora and Spike had used about how easy it was to start and how it would take care of all the essential electrical needs of the hotel if power was ever interrupted. Which, of course, "would never happen." The four hours on the machine's meter seemed to naively confirm their story.

That we were without a generator during hurricane season was not a good thought. The $1,100 and four months to replace the coil that had melted in the little fire beat the heck out of a new generator's price of $3,700. We'd risk it.

Joan heard us coming and made a quick mental adjustment, seeing me arriving via the tradesman's stairway with bags in tow, followed by the Saint Croix version of the Mod Squad: Reuben, the hot mortician, and the senior-citizen companion. He had introduced himself as Jack—"her chaperone."

The check-in to their prepaid room consisted of nothing more than handing them the key to Upper Love, one of our nicest rooms and the proud possessor of a new $1,300 air-conditioner unit purchased earlier in the week.

The mortician was in a hurry to dump her things and anxious to introduce herself to her potential employer. That was the last thing we would see her do that made any sense for a job applicant on a tropical island.

During the six minutes the duo was inside getting settled, our friendship with Reuben began. He was not a happy camper. He had silently waited at the airport since 11:00 a.m. with no word from the prospective mortician. They had been due in at 11:10 a.m. on the first flight from Miami. Actual arrival had been close to 4:00 p.m. on the third and last daily flight.

While I had grown impatient at the Pink, poor Reuben had killed time at the airport. When a driver gets an assignment on the island to pick up guest A at point B, he does that. He does not call back to headquarters every twenty minutes, asking what he should do. He guts it out.

Cal Coolidge and Joan Coolidge

He would have certainly been accustomed to the heat as, like most less-modern Caribbean airports, Henry J. Rohlsen International was cooled only by the rumored constant breeze. In September at midisland, six miles away from the water, that breeze was plenty warm—and it wasn't constant. The cabbies and minibus drivers could only find refuge under the metal overhangs outside baggage claim, where they were known to improvise a low table and engage in spirited domino games between arrivals.

A second option would be to drive about five hundred yards outside the airport gate and turn left at the mural of native son and NBA star Tim Duncan onto the grounds of the dustiest horse track in the northern hemisphere. Under the metal grandstand in place for once-monthly racing on blazing Sunday afternoons were a series of old-style TVs hanging on metal brackets. This gave about thirty underemployed Crucians the opportunity to bet on the ponies running in New York, Miami, or Los Angeles via simulcast. On a couple of my worst days, I had tried to entertain myself there. The clientele was not much different than what I'd have found at Rosecroft Raceway, across the Potomac from our former home in Alexandria. They were all characters, to say the least.

How Reuben had spent those five hours was never revealed, but it was clear he hadn't hit the Pick 6 at Santa Anita and was agitated. Over the next six days, agitation would escalate to frustration. It took four days for

Reuben to tell us that our guests had missed the early Miami flight because of a serious case of intoxication. I had missed the signs completely.

CHAPTER 29

——— ❧ ———

Thursday Evening, Our Night Out (Cal)

WITH OUR IMPORTANT guest off to dinner with her host and "chaperone," we saw no reason to stay at the hotel that evening. By mid-September, we had developed a nice pattern of going out on Thursday nights. Our few other guests seemed self-sufficient, and we always made sure they were comfortable with us away for a few hours.

An Italian restaurant called the Cultured Pelican was set high on the hills of the east end of Saint Croix. It offered a two-for-one dinner special on Thursdays that attracted the local businesspeople who could get away long enough to relax for a couple of hours.

Our group usually included a guest or two whom we were enjoying having at the hotel and who appreciated being taken on a short road trip. In this category were Joan's hyperactive and always-broke friend Sue, the KraZi Stans on occasion, perhaps one of the pilots from Seaborne Airlines, or Alaska Sam (who bore no similarity to Lazy Sam).

Tonight, it was Sue, who was on the island to find herself while working a thankless job in the public-school system after a painful divorce back in Utah.

And there was Kendra, our loyal business traveler who hailed from Maine. She was an IT consultant tasked with making sense of and improving the government's very outdated computer system used to occasionally collect taxes.

Johnnie, a tall, well-built guy who was a tenant of the Stans waited tables at the restaurant. We always treated him well with a strong tip. We'd become regulars on Thursdays, allowing Maurice, the owner, to act as if we were long-lost friends. I was "somebody" there. I liked being somebody, even it was the owner of a half-full hotel with no generator during hurricane season.

The meal was excellent, complete with the mysteriously good Caesar salad—mysterious because we knew the poor quality of ingredients we normal shoppers had such trouble finding fresh. We all laughed our way through the meal, enjoying a classic sunset preceded by multiple rainbows off to the northeast in the direction of Tortola. Living the dream on a tropical island was feeling pretty good this evening.

It may have been 10:30 p.m. by the time our well-lubricated group made its way back to Christiansted, past the Buccaneer Hotel complex and the fort guarding the harbor. I was the designated driver, and the ladies had taken full advantage. They had had a nice evening. So far.

Back at the hotel, our other guests that week were all "classics"—and totally individual parties with no common thread save they were all enjoying their stays at the Pink Fancy and on Saint Croix. To return from our night out to find that spontaneous combustion can occur among eight strangers with a love for cheap alcohol had not been on the agenda—at least, not on mine.

When we parked the Ford Escape that served as the hotel's official vehicle on the street below and unloaded ourselves, the voices coming from seventeen steps high above us and under the canopy around our pool were spirited. Sue was stimulated by this; Joan was immediately worried. Kendra was probably pissed that her nearby room was within earshot and that sleep would be impossible. I wanted to avoid the whole scene.

As always, Peanut and Sally greeted us at the top of the seventeen steps of stone. The journey up the steps was made more interesting by the property's National Historical Record plaque, but we didn't take the time to read it on this trip.

The objects that came into sight as we ascended the seventeen steps, other than the heads of seven guests who had not been with us at dinner, were the tops of a plethora of wine bottles, followed by the slightly shorter beer bottles, then cans both vertical and horizontal scattered around our large breakfast table under the canopy. The shouting didn't pause for an instant as we four emerged onto the patio and pool level. These folks were engaged in debate.

The exception was Paula, already recognized as escapee from reality in California and a leading consumer of cheap wine and free rum at the Pink. She was slumped forward, head down, with a computer laptop on her knees, passed out or close to it. She had been around long enough to confess all to Joan about several miserable relationships and cut-short careers. She had also, however, been observant enough over the past few days to know where Joan stashed our personal wine. She must have declared an alcohol emergency when the crowd's own supply ran low. Several liter bottles of Joan's pinot grigio had now been victims of assault.

Bob, the thrice-married-by-thirty insurance adjuster working on fourteen-year-old claims from Hurricane Hugo (circa 1989), seemed close to crossing the line with the miniskirted mortician. The "chaperone," Jack, was trying to reinsert himself between his seriously impaired charge and Bob. Jack was about to explode.

The entire group, the members of which hailed from four different rooms, had obviously been at it for a while. "It" might have started elsewhere on the island and probably separately at one or more of the various happy hours along the boardwalk, but upon returning to the Pink, they had continued with a vengeance. It was a bit surprising that the job candidate had gotten such a running start at a first dinner with her prospective employer, but hey...we were on the islands, not in suburban America.

There was a minimum of seventy bottles open, and empty bottles and cans were scattered on the large glass breakfast table. I did the math. There were a total of seven people around the table. We were talking close to alcohol-poisoning levels for all of them!

Joan could handle this one. I retreated into the utility closet-cum-family room-cum-TV room, shutting the door to the office and beginning to search for a baseball game on our satellite TV network. What a jerk.

Joan, who can temporarily hold a really miserable series of events inside without screaming better than your average citizen, started to work the problem by rousing Paula. "Shit-faced" would have been a complimentary way to describe her condition. "It is time to go back to your room, Paula," said Joan calmly, with Sue helping to steady the laptop in case she obeyed.

"Gotta go inside," mumbled Paula. She had to pee, and she knew the owner's quarters had two toilets that were much closer than her quarters on street level. She made a move for ours through the outdoor kitchen beyond the microsized office, opening the door I had shut when I disappeared. Joan was on her tail. As Joan passed, her eyes bored a hole through me that said, "You asshole." I knew that look. I jumped out of the recliner, but rising to stop Paula had no effect. She was not going back to her room to pee.

The voices outside were suddenly at war. Bottles flew over the breakfast table, and chairs were pushed back, screeching across the cement floor under the canopy. Bob and the sixty-five-year-old chaperone had had enough of each other. Somebody connected with a body blow.

From inside, where I was about to take an offensive charge from a ready-to-piss Paula, a pissed-off Joan, and a cautiously laughing Sue, it sounded like the verbal scene by the pool had become physical. The yelling quickly overtook the pushing, but no one ended up submerged in the nearby pool. Then, quiet...had they retreated to their rooms?

Trying to reason with a drunk has few upsides. Paula was headed for Joan's bathroom just off the owner's spacious bedroom area. I generally used the steamy bathroom connected to the utility room, but Paula barreled right past that one and was quickly behind the door of Joan's. Things were suddenly silent. Joan had retreated to the pool area to see what damage was being done, while I contemplated the extradition of Paula as Sue observed nearby, just for sport.

Back out around the pool, Joan was watching the group scatter. It wasn't clear if the young mortician had gone in door number one with Bob or had been dragged into her suite with the chaperone of senior status. In either case, there were no bottles hitting the tiles.

I, being more than slightly afraid of Joan's temper, turned to Sue. I wasn't about to go into a bathroom to retrieve a female. Sue, after all, had a background in psychology...or was it physiology? Anyway, she could be counted on to put a collar hold on Paula, and besides, their rooms were side by side downstairs. I could get two of them off to bed in one shot, and I'd be back to watching baseball posthaste.

After a couple of minutes of discussing strategy for dealing with Paula, who was surely facedown on the ceramic tile in the bathroom, I opened the door. She was neither horizontal nor vertical. She was wedged between the shower and the sink, alongside the porcelain princess, with soggy panties around her ankles. It appeared that she hadn't made it there in time.

Paula's upper torso, while her hands still grabbed the laptop—which was precariously close to the toilet—was at a forty-degree angle to the wall, according to my mental protractor. I got a hand under the laptop as Sue used her foot to inch Paula's panties back over her knees. Paula, in a purely involuntary nerve reaction, finished the job—at least over the left cheek.

Sue and I propped her up (or maybe lifted her) so that feet at least scraped tile as they exited the bathroom through the owner's suite and back through the always steamy-hot, hundred-square-foot utility room-office-TV room that served as my nightly escape from reality.

As the trio made their way, Paula suddenly had a flashback to her days working at a Footlocker, apparently. She bent over and quickly picked up a pair of my shoes—size-ten-and-a-half, D-width, all-purpose cross-training sneakers. Her grasp was tight. "Paula, those are mine," I suggested. The grip tightened, and she was now building steam under her own power. Oh, no, she insisted, these shoes were hers.

Sue pointed out to Paula that she was wearing her own white Dockers. That had no effect. My only hope was to recover the shoes at room cleaning the next day when

Paula went after liquid groceries—typically, that was before noon.

The priority was now getting Paula to her room, with a fifty-fifty chance that she'd emerge from her drunken coma in time to make it to happy hour tomorrow at four. She'd never recall this night's activities, and she'd wear Joan out again with stories of how her exes never understood her and that she'd never been much of a party girl back in California when some bitch mother complained to the board of education that she'd smelled of booze at a parent-teacher conference.

The adventures of the mortician's visit were just beginning, however.

CHAPTER 30

—— ✿ ——

The Seven-Day
Mystery Tour (Cal)

THE CLEANUP FROM the spontaneous party overloaded the trash can labeled "glass recycling." Seventy-nine bottles and cans, to be exact. There was no recycling on the island. The label on the trash can was only there to pacify the ecotourists, who could be zealots.

I had all that done before Joan emerged at 7:20 a.m. for her customary sanity walk. She maintained her mental and physical health by power walking on the boardwalk up to Gallows Bay, past the bright-yellow fort that protected Christiansted Harbor and had once imprisoned Alexander Hamilton's mother while he, as a teenager, learned the ins and out of global commerce as a weights-and-measures guy and kept the books for a group of rich local merchants.

I was well onto the first deleafing of the pool and servicing the early risers' rooms by the time she returned, a healthy sweat on her brow and soaking her white Pink Fancy T-shirt. "The Pink Fancy: The Jewel of the Caribbean" was emblazoned on the back.

It was relatively easy to keep an eye on the guests as they departed after grabbing coffee and bagels at our outdoor-kitchen serving area. The employed were first to leave, unless we happened to have a hyperactive triathlete in-house.

By 2:00 p.m., neither Joan nor I had seen the mortician or chaperone emerge. Maybe they had gone out super early? Not likely, considering the state they had been in at eleven last night.

It was about then that our seven days of "What the hell are they doing in there?" questions began. This was, after all, a tropical island, and the weather was perfect. Wouldn't you want to get out and soak up the sun?

An ear to the door of Upper Love did not reveal any wild sex—or, frankly, anything—going on. The TV was off; no light showed through the louvered doors. Wouldn't you think they'd sleep it off by the pool or at least get out to see the island?

Now, it is quite likely that veteran hoteliers would be able to just ignore this behavior, but it was troubling to rookies like Joan and me. At 4:00 p.m., my curiosity got the better of me, and I tapped on the door. A male moan was heard—not one of pleasure; just one that said, "What the hell time is it, anyway?"

"Do you want us to make up the room?" I asked through the door, wishing I had let sleeping dogs lie.

"No," came the faint reply. There was no evidence of consciousness from the female mortician.

That was the extent of day number two. We weren't able to pinpoint why we should give a damn if they came out, but it sure seemed strange. It wasn't like they'd taken groceries in with them. What were those two doing?

Sundays, some guests sleep late. We hadn't had one before who just slept. There was no evidence whatsoever that either had left the room. We supposed that after a few years of owning a hotel, this wouldn't trouble us, but we still felt like we were having guests at our home. Under such circumstances, wasn't this just a little inconsiderate? I reminded Joan that this was a seven-day, full-price, paid-in-advance reservation. We didn't have many of those in mid-September.

Reuben, last seen on Thursday at check-in, showed up at the gate promptly at 1:30 p.m. on Monday. I was pretty sure I had seen Jack darting down the steps to the street earlier in the morning, but I had not seen him return. There had been no visual on the good-looking mortician since Thursday night. I passed that intelligence on to Reuben as he walked in the gate and up the seventeen stone steps to pool level. He was hiding some anger inside.

Reuben had been "on call" should our cross between Sleeping Beauty and Cruella de Vil want to tour the island or maybe check out local real estate, presupposing that Mr. Shanks was going to hire her. He hadn't appreciated hanging around waiting for a call, but here he was, apparently on time to meet them, as had been discussed on Thursday when he'd brought the two back from dinner at Mr. Shanks's.

He paced around for a minute before I invited him to sit down. "Reuben, my man, this a strange one...Have a seat." Reuben explained how Ms. Mortician had hinted that she'd be fine over the weekend but that she had promised his boss that she'd come tour the "home" (as in funeral) Monday afternoon.

At first, Reuben didn't want me to call the room to inform them he was there, but after forty-five minutes, during which his murmuring softly built to frustration over Thursday's pickup at the airport, he started to weaken. "They are drunks of the worst kind, I assure you." Reuben spoke in the more formal West Indian English that American tourists often find startling.

"Does Mr. Shanks know this?"

"No. He likes her. She acted nothing more obvious than happy when they met on Thursday," Rueben reported.

"You must tell Mr. Shanks," I suggested.

"It is not my place," he responded.

"But what if he hires her?" The thought of being assigned to this pair as a full-time driver must have passed through Reuben's mind. It was a scary thought.

It was pushing 2:30 p.m. when I told him, "Look, I am going to call the room." This time, he did not object.

The phone rang four times before it was knocked off the hook and retrieved from the floor. The chaperone answered. He had returned! He was redefining the word "chaperone," I thought as I heard him say, "What?"

"Hey, listen. Reuben, your driver, is here and says he was supposed to pick you up this afternoon. It is Monday, by the way. He has been here about an hour. Are you and your charge going to be ready to go soon?"

"No, not today. Tell him we'll call him." This was the worst of all responses to relay to Reuben. *Click.* The phone was hung up with a flourish.

Thus ended contact with Love Station Zebra, or whatever the hell Upper Love had turned into. What the hell were those two doing in there?

CHAPTER 31

—— ❦ ——

Tuesday (Cal)

SOMETHING HAD TO crack on Tuesday. We thought it might be the four-poster bed, but we hoped it might be the door during daylight hours. Reuben had tipped us off that Mr. Shanks, still uninformed of this woman's true nature, had called her directly on her cell phone on Monday evening. Apparently, she had reported her love for the island, the Pink Fancy, and all things STX. Driver Reuben was not sure that Mr. Shanks had bought the story, but he was still not willing to reveal the truth unless asked. The funeral-home business must have a lot of secrets, and perhaps Reuben thought a breach of confidentiality with a client might be a roadblock to career advancement.

We did learn that the mortician and chaperone had committed to join the Shanks family at their stately home on the hill for dinner that evening. His wife Jules was known to provide humor into any event held at their compound. The steady death business, not to mention the twenty-five-year political career of the now-dead patriarch, had afforded the leading black family a very nice lifestyle on Saint Croix.

Seven that evening was pickup time, Reuben let me know. So, the lady mortician would make an appearance tonight, and we would survey the condition of our best room while our guests were out. Joan was anxious and ready to pounce if she found any of the antique furniture damaged. What the hell had they been doing in there for five days?

It all happened in a flash. Reuben rang the bell at street level. I buzzed him in, and almost simultaneously, the mortician emerged. How could this be? She was completely put together—she had on a midthigh skirt, spiked heels on her feet, and a colorful and tasteful blouse. Her hair was very presentable, and there was no sign of bruises, dark bags under her eyes, or bloodshot peepers. She was checking out as a solid 8.7 to 9.1 on the infamous pretty-girl scale. She looked great.

With Jack behind her, she glided across the tiled poolside deck. He knew his place, apparently. Jack did acknowledge in his eye contact with me that she was a bit unusual and seemed to know that we'd been troubled by the entire weird stay. The pair moved down the seventeen steps of stone, out the wrought-iron gate, and into the black limo (freshly cleaned after this afternoon's trip up to the Crucian burial grounds on official business).

The highly anticipated but dreaded moment had arrived for us innkeepers. Joan was through the bedroom door as the limo pulled away, and a low "Oh my God" came out as she stepped on something round before the light came on. It was a bottle. An empty bottle. I followed her in. The bed was in one piece, the art still on the walls, the blinds drawn, and the storm shutters pulled closed.

The furniture was, for some unknown reason, away from the walls, and the floor was completely covered—I mean, completely!—with bottles. Liquor, wine, beer—all empty. I saw makeup jars among the mess. Clothes were scattered everywhere, which begged the question: when (and where) had she worn those clothes?

The count on the bottles was worthy of a multifunction calculator—there were certainly well over a hundred. They were randomly strewn everywhere: around the bathtub, on the dresser, under the bed, and there were even a few intact ones, ready for another day.

It was hard to find a place to put our feet as we investigated. Joan started to pick up. I suggested, while fearing her wrath, "Listen, this a fucking mess, but they leave tomorrow. Why do it twice?" Joan was fuming. They had violated her home—or at least she felt that way.

The gathering at the Shanks' family villa on the hill went past midnight. There had been no sign of the pair's return, but by eight fifteen on Wednesday morning, the assault on Upper Love was over. Once again, looking completely put together and normal, chaperone in tow, the mortician departed. She was never seen again.

When that woman dies, no embalming fluid will be required.

We had made a friend in Reuben. He and I had talked baseball; he was a huge Atlanta Braves fan. He was delighted when I gave him the authentic Braves jersey that I had been given by the minor-league team, the Richmond Braves, a couple of years earlier. As one of five folks they'd found with presidential names, I had been asked to throw out the first pitch on an opening day—the ninetieth anniversary of William Howard Taft being the first president to do so. Reuben had earned that jersey. We would see him occasionally on the streets of Christiansted, and he was always wearing the bright-white jersey with a back that read "Coolidge 30."

Joan developed the theory that the mortician wasn't one at all, but a vampire. After all, what better job was there for a vampire than to drain people's blood legally? When the pair checked out, I charged them for smoking in the room and pretty much let them know that they would never stay with us again. Then we brought the huge trash can up from the basement and filled it until it overflowed.

—— ❧ ——

CHAPTER 32

Grocery Shopping on the Island (Cal)

ON SAINT CROIX, you learn quickly that the food boat arrives on Wednesday. It takes a bit longer to realize that this means it left San Juan on Monday night and probably left Tampa or Miami on Friday last. The fruits and vegetables might well have been fresh then.

Moving to a tropical island, you'd expect that fresh fruit would be plentiful. Correct...if you can live on carambola fruit, otherwise known as star fruit—a somewhat bitter-tasting, juicy mouthful if you find one fresh off a tree in someone's yard or alongside the golf course, which is appropriately named Carambola Golf Club.

A vegetable farm was known to exist on the east end of Saint Croix. Our two visits there revealed a weak inventory of not much. But it was organic!

Wednesday afternoons, my duty was to leave the hotel (a prison-break-like moment) and drive to PayLow, our version of Costco, and stock up for the coming week. This involved first cruising through the extensive alcohol section, which offered the only bargains in the entire store. Within days of our arrival, we had broken the code on why island drinks were always so strong. Alcohol itself was about half the cost of mixers, sodas, and juices. Honest to God...Tanqueray Gin was—what? About thirty-eight dollars a liter on the mainland? How about $5.95 on Saint Croix? Cruzan Rum (our homegrown favorite) was cheaper than bottled water. In fact, it wasn't even close.

It wasn't the booze that you were anxious to stock up on. It was the fruit, vegetables, and juices that your body craved more than you could have imagined. The stories of ancient sailors dying of scurvy were becoming easier to believe after a few months of laboring in the Caribbean sun. There was something about that experience that sucked the nutrients right out of your body.

If I had five or six rooms to clean on a good morning when we had guests, the heat and humidity I encountered in rooms with little moving air would cause me to sweat through at least three T-shirts. By break time, my shorts and underwear could be wrung out when I finally sat down, which I would get to do at about twelve thirty. By that point, despite hydrating with bottled water multiple times during the morning, I would find myself craving fruit juices. I could easily drain a half gallon of cranberry-apple juice without hardly taking time to breathe.

Upon hitting the bottled-juice section of PayLow, in a move that was necessary but that I knew I would regret when coming up those seventeen steps of stone from street level to the kitchen and pool level, I would load gallons of orange juice, cranberry juice, guava juice, and a single half gallon of milk into the rapidly overflowing shopping cart.

It was then on to the vegetables, in the unsqueezed-and-solid form. Recall that they had all just arrived, but they already had an appearance that would prompt you to ask for the manager at your local Safeway back home. The lettuce was slightly wilted, with a yellowish-brown tint starting to take over the edges.

Today, I spied cucumbers! This was a treat that didn't happen every week. I loved cucumbers. I'd raised them whenever we had a small garden plot back in Virginia. What a summer treat they had been. You could eat them chilled in spears or add them to a salad. When the supply exceeded demand, they were wonderful thinly sliced and pickled a bit in vinegar accented with a few onion slices and a dash of pepper. My mother always had a midsize stainless-steel bowl of them in the refrigerator from July through the first frost that never ran low. What didn't get devoured by the family of six would be seriously pickled for later use in crocks that had served the family for generations in New England.

The fresh Saint Croix versions didn't look bad—for Saint Croix. They were only marginally soft. In fact, they were pretty darn firm, it seemed. I scooped up four, all intended for my personal consumption.

I couldn't forget to pick up sweet potatoes and bananas, no matter what the condition. Joan had adopted a resident turtle, Maggie, who seemed to be happily single, on the grounds of the Pink Fancy. Joan and Maggie had developed a daily feeding pattern that may surprise you. We would call, "Maggie! Maggie, time for dinner!" and within three minutes, she would emerge from the jungle-like brush that skirted the side of our little old school-house building. Maggie would slowly chomp down on several pieces of sweet potato—cooked, of course—and bananas that Joan had cut up for her. Joan had a history of being loved by animals all her life and was the perfect pet mom. She understood that no matter what the pet, they loved routines. She also made a pattern of routine in all she did. That was a comforting thing to her own children as well.

By the time I reached the checkout line, five carts deep on Wednesdays, my beloved cucumbers didn't look quite as firm as I had thought they were thirty minutes earlier. How could this be?

It was stifling hot, that was how. By the time I'd ventured across the steamy parking lot and loaded close to three hundred pounds of liquid into the vehicle, the cucumbers were fading. I decided to put the cukes on the front seat with me. Some air conditioning would make it up to them, I theorized. They would need special supervision, if not consumption, to make it back to the Pink Fancy. About two miles from the hotel, I decided not to risk it. I ate two of the cucumbers, skin and all. They would never have made it to the refrigerator.

We never did understand how residents struggled to have fresh veggies and fruits, yet you could eat at any of the truly good restaurants on the island and be served wonderful salads and fruit bowls. How did they do that? It was as if they had some kind of freshness-chemical spray. I hated to think what it might be.

PART 3

Reality Check

CHAPTER 33

—— ❧ ——

This Just Isn't Going to Work (Cal)

ONCE YOU COME to realize that you have undertaken something that could have a devastating impact on your life, you have a very hard time focusing on anything except your exit strategy. I had come to the conclusion probably prematurely—like the day I received the closing papers and saw that the hotel hadn't *really* sold since 1971.

Four months into the venture, discussions with other entrepreneurs on the island were comforting, in a way.

"Cal, you need to see how high season goes—you will feel differently."

"When would that be?" I asked.

"Some years, as early as Christmas week. Others, mid-January."

"And it lasts till…?"

"Well, that is hard to say, but hopefully through most of April."

Holy shit.

I am not a private person. I felt better only when I confided my growing fear that I had blown it by embarking on this walk on the wild side. I confided in my newfound golf partner Hugh that I was losing sleep. I didn't admit that I had been close to puking and having suicidal thoughts as I swept mango leaves out of the pool for the fifth time yesterday. Drowning is a horrifying way to go, but I'd actually thought through how I'd chain myself to one of the very heavy sundeck chairs around the pool and fall in, sinking to the bottom with only about three minutes to endure the struggle.

That ending was starting to seem easier than telling Joan that all my optimism and big plans for success as an innkeeper, serving rum punches to friends and tourists as they told us how lucky we were to have "the life" as we lived out our years in the sun of Saint Croix, was turning out to be a pipe dream. That discussion was going to be one of the hardest things I had ever faced.

Without a way out, I truly was beginning to fear that we could find ourselves marooned, burning our way through the safety net of savings that we both counted on to live well into retirement. It wasn't like there was some high-dollar pension waiting for us. My main career in the defense business had ended at age forty-nine, way too early to qualify for a retirement salary. What we had, we had—just that, and the prospect of both of us finding real work for another fifteen years if it ran out.

Joan had bought into the dream and was, like always, head down, doing her part to accomplish the daily tasks necessary to make the venture a success. She's never been the type to quit. She had not even begun to worry about cash flow, low occupancy, constant repairs, or $3,000 monthly electrical bills. I was holding it in, but I could see the handwriting on the wall.

It was Labor Day weekend, just three months after our arrival and the end of the beach season back home, when I said, "We need to go to the beach today." It wasn't like we had a crowd at the Pink Fancy. In fact, apparently, everyone was at his or her own beach on the mainland. We were empty.

Cane Bay was a beach that Crucians and tourists alike knew was world class: a bit of a half-moon shape to it, green mountains in the background, and the renowned "wall" just five hundred feet away. There were also some of the best fish tacos anywhere if you walked across the road to the Cane Bay Reef House. When you drove North Shore Road past Cane Bay, you encountered a hill called the "Beast." The Beast was doable in your vehicle—barely.

The Beast had earned its name in the annual Saint Croix 70.3-mile IRONMAN Triathlon held each year in early May. As you drove up the Beast, images of a dreadful dragon painted on the blacktop looked as if the dragon were on a wall outside your windshield, not on the road below. It is that steep. On the way down, the person in the passenger seat would be grasping the dashboard and hanging on for dear life. How in hell the triathletes on bicycles pumped their way up it midway through the grueling test of endurance each May was beyond imagination. Those athletes were amazing. "Lungs on legs" is how I referred to them.

At the top of the hill on a clear day, you could occasionally see the islands of Vieques off Puerto Rico's southeast coast, said to be seventy miles away. It would be a perfect spot to see the green flash.

"The wall" attracted divers looking for a spot where one could walk into the clearest blue water and descend into the black abyss of a canyon that separated the continental plate of South America from the North American plate. The wall plunged to depths of thirteen thousand feet right there. It was easy to swim out over it with just snorkel gear. You could go from clear blue against white sand to the blackest of black in a matter of yards. It was kind of scary. But not as scary as having to tell your wife you might have messed up her life—again.

CHAPTER 34

—— ✐ ——

Cane Bay (Cal)

IT MIGHT HAVE been a strategy of mine to get Joan away from the hotel, where she'd feel obligated to get back to work on the tiles that were showing their daily encroachment of black mold. It might also have been to give her a feeling of freedom and carefreeness that a day at the beach provided. More likely, I wanted her in a public setting where at least there would be witnesses to my impending murder if her inherited temper got the best of her.

I decided not to wait for perfect.

On the very hot and steamy road past the Hovensa Petroleum refinery, on the south side of midisland, I started the conversation with the age-old lead-in to serious stuff: "We need to talk."

A number of not-pleasant conversations had been started that way over the past thirty-two years—mostly by Joan, and mostly when I had gotten myself a bit out of control. We weren't the best at difficult conversations, but we had faced them and survived them. Any married couple can think of moments when the shit hit the fan. Perhaps the measure of a truly lifelong relationship is having the staying power to survive those.

"About what?" Joan responded.

"This is just not going to work...the hotel...the whole idea is crazy," I blurted out, getting it over with and onto the proverbial table.

"What are you talking about? We just got here! How do you know this already? You were so certain that everything was going to be easy!"

"I know, and maybe it can be, but I have become convinced that we have ourselves in big trouble," I added, avoiding eye contact by gazing across the scorched grass around the refinery as we continued the drive westward. "Joan, there are so many things we have no control over. That is what has hit me. We can have the cutest little hotel on Saint Croix, but if freakin' American Airlines decides to triple the fare to get here, it is like turning off the tap of tourists. And that has already happened. Not to mention the weather, which since our arrival in June has been sweltering. You can see how anxious even friends have been to visit. Here we are, in the midst of hurricane season, with no generator and no wind insurance. And I have a fungus growing on my ass from being wet sixteen hours a day. I don't panic easily, but I am scared shitless that this is not for us."

During the closing process, all the arrangements that could have been made to mitigate risk, liability, and fire had been procured for the compound of four buildings. This all ran $14,000 annually, a tad more than your basic homeowner's policy back home. When the topic of hurricane insurance had come up, we learned that people here "self-insure." I had pressed on the topic and actually did request a quotation, which was arranged via Lloyd's of London (that should give you a hint). The quotation was a quick lesson in why folks self-insure. We were dealing with a facility worth less than $1.5 million that had somehow not been destroyed in a hurricane since its 1780 construction. The quote was $34,500 annually—and oh, by the way, came with a $500,000 deductible. We'd self-insure.

The rest of the trip to Cane Bay was fifteen miles of silence with a few interjections by Joan and not very good answers by me.

"What about the due diligence you kept saying you had done? Are you saying we are going to go broke? Jesus, we just got here. You know things will be better in the high season."

The high-season thought had been comforting as I had tried to meet and get to know other business owners, but I'd allowed thoughts of full capacity of fourteen rented rooms at rack rate of about $150, times thirty days per month, to form my expectations. It just wasn't to be.

In the "due diligence" I had done, I had found data with the board of tourism that said occupancy on the island ran at 28 percent, the same figure the appraiser had used. I'd discounted it as "must be wrong," preferring to think that it had to be understated due to cash business and tax evasion. I was learning quickly that it was reality—the long off-season and Saint Croix having a lot of competition from destinations that were newer and flashier in the public's eye.

Saint Croix's heyday was behind it. In the fifties, sixties, and early seventies, it had been the hotspot destination for both Americans and Europeans, powered by a better airport and its multinational background. Planeloads of Dutch tourists had descended upon Saint

Croix weekly in the not-so-distant past, not to mention the nonstop flights from New York that had given the island a reputation as the place to go for the winter getaway.

That all came to a screeching end in 1972 with the Fountain Valley Massacre. Islanders want desperately to forget this turning point in the island's history. You would think that after forty-plus years, they might have. "It never happened before, and it has never happened since" was about all we were offered by our real estate broker, Mary, who was actually terrific when she took us to lunch as we toured the island on the original trip to "just look around."

She explained that there had been a murder...well, in fact, *eight* murders...at the bar of the clubhouse of the Robert Trent Jones-designed Fountain Valley Golf Course, now renamed the Carambola Golf Club.

It all happened on September 6, 1972, when five disaffected locals came to the course to get some spending money off a group of golfers. Details after forty-plus years are hard to come by—but the robbery had gone bad. The golfers resisted the intruders, resulting in gunfire.

It was a one-sided affair, as it is a rare golfer who plans ahead for self-defense on the course. The foursome from the Miami area were all killed, as were four employees of the club working in the bar area. Seven victims were white, and one was a local African Caribbean.

Needless to say, Saint Croix's reputation was soiled, and it only got worse as the plight of the murderers was sensationalized in the *New York Times* by the radical defense attorney William Kunstler. According to the surviving businesspeople, who did their best never to talk about the incident, Kunstler "tried the case in the *New York Times*." He turned what most believed was a botched robbery attempt, to one in which persecuted, lower-class Caribbean African Americans were trying to get their share from rich, white, carefree golfers. He made it a racial battle that targeted noble Vietnam veterans.

Mary chose to mention this story when we were actually sitting in the exact spot where it had occurred. Perhaps her thinking was, we could clearly see with our own eyes that the bloodstains were long gone, and the peaceful setting in the shade of mango trees, where there is always a breeze, had long ago returned to the country club. The peaceful setting had returned; we could see that. The question remained: Had tourists returned?

Attorney Kunstler had not succeeded in getting his clients off for their crime but he had done great damage to the island's reputation.

In a strange twist to this awful crime we learned, while living on the island, that the main perpetrator was later returned to the island to stand trial in a civil suit late in 1984. On the commercial flight back to prison on the mainland the flight was hijacked to Havana Cuba despite having a US Marshall hired guard on board . He has not been seen since.

CHAPTER 35

Taking Action (Cal)

THIS WAS NOT the first crisis I had had to find my way out of, but this one was going to require more creativity than just apologizing to Joan and claiming it would never happen again. I'd already made a secret visit to Mary and her partner to get their opinions on how to get out of the venture.

The real estate partners were both compassionate ladies who had certainly seen newbies panic before. But they were also strong defenders of the island and wanted to see it progress. They joined the entrepreneurs and business owners who begged me to see things through a high season or two: "Things will look different to you with a few months of success under your belts."

Veterans on Saint Croix were genuinely happy to see a couple like Joan and me arrive. It certainly gave them hope that Saint Croix was turning the corner and that new money was arriving. Most, wisely, were not allowing themselves to worry about the uncontrollable factors.

It was enough for many of them just to be warm. When, on one of my more dejected days, I asked the owner of a jewelry shop along the boardwalk how she could handle this heat (it was a sunny July day at noon, ninety-five degrees, and 95 percent humidity), she replied, "I will never shovel snow again." As I continued on my steamy boardwalk trek that day, I came to realize that if you placed a high priority on never seeing the white stuff again, whatever Saint Croix and the tropical heat threw at you might all be worth it. I had actually enjoyed snowy days.

The real estate people advised against trying to flip a property on the island, especially a small hotel, in anything resembling a short time. That was just foolish dreaming.

A sinking feeling went through me as I confronted the harsh reality of digging myself out of this hole. Actually, it was more like an already-sunken feeling.

CHAPTER 36

***

There Must Be Somebody (Cal)

"Wasn't there anyone else who had come close to making a bid before we arrived?" I asked on my next visit, after promising himself I would not bother the ladies for at least a week.

"Not while I was working on it," Mary responded.

"No inquiries, even? Certainly you had interest in your Internet ads?"

"Yes, but they were mostly dreamers who could never pull it off. You get that a lot when you live in paradise, especially during the dead of winter. Those types see the upside but then realize they have commitments at home, and most don't come close to having the money. They feel stuck, but they don't have any options, really."

I was for the first time regretting that I hadn't let either of those factors slow us down.

With no prospect of a quick sale on the horizon, high season four months away, and routine advertising failing to attract more than the occasional guest who wanted a discount, I reminded myself that my career had been made in sales and marketing. I had been good at it—not because I had known more about the products I was selling than the next person but because I knew people, loved to meet and talk with them, and was authentic when I had the opportunity to get in front of the customer. Most people liked me and quickly trusted me.

I certainly did not know more about the hotel and hospitality business. But I've never been fearful of getting out and "hitting the bricks." I visited every law office in Christiansted, always with the question in the back of my mind: *Why are there so many law offices?* There were more than thirty in little old Christiansted, Saint Croix.

I asked each to consider the Pink Fancy when they had business associates in town. Other than a few maybes should they ever bring in an expert witness, it seemed that all the legal battles were law firm A versus law firm B. That explained it.

While getting to know people, I could make it interesting, telling them about the hotel and about our venture here on the island. And I'd always ask for the sale—an often-forgotten element of the sales call I'd learned by watching others.

Not only did I call on law offices but other businesses and even the National Guard commander: we needed guests, and guys on deployment would be the best—captive and busy for two weeks at a time, minimum. I could only imagine what a house full of recruits paying the "government rate" would do for my attitude. (Of course we had a government rate.)

I made a successful call to the nearby Seaborne Airlines office three hundred yards away on the boardwalk. They were a growing concern headed by a young entrepreneur, Omar Oreclik, who also had a fabulous hot sauce called Anna's that he was trying to bottle, market, and export. I bonded with Omar and perhaps appealed to his compassion for others struggling on the island.

Seaborne had a class of eight new pilots coming in for a three-week training class the next month. A visit by his secretary was set up for the next day, as she was empowered to find them lodging. The rum punches flowed during that visit!

We loved having the pilots and did our best to be kind to them. We hosted a pig-roast dinner, inviting local businesspeople for them to mingle with. The single ladies were the most popular with the young pilots.

One evening, as dusk settled in, I suggested to the pilots that cocktails would be served if we all convened on the third-level deck that had a view all the way to Tortola. We'd be able to see the lights on Saint Thomas and Saint John as well. They were strong volunteers.

For Joan and me, this was "the good life," or the "living the dream" part of the whole experience—the way you'd like life to be all the time.

That evening, Joan concocted the Pink Fancy punch in a vat, combining four-dollar Cruzan rum, mango flavoring, and equal parts mango, guava, and orange juices from their eight-dollar bottles. I scooped up a three-gallon bucket with ice from the ice machine, barely able to see in the fading light of the day.

As the guys worked their way through the fourth and fifth rum punch, they told story after story, using both hands in airplane formation as pilots incessantly do: "There I was..." came out time and time again. Some stories were scary; some were funny. Many ended with close calls. And the next one was always just a little better.

The guys needed the break after a nine-hour classroom day learning about the sixteen-passenger Sea Otter aircraft they would be island-hopping in six hours a day or more at entry-level pilot wages. When the last handful of ice was retrieved from the bucket, signaling the end of the evening was near, a "holy shit, look at this" came out of Marvin's mouth. When I had filled the bucket with ice in the dark, unnoticed at the bottom had been a nine-inch iguana, who had just experienced an hour of arctic weather. The poor guy was living the cold-blooded life that reptiles have. He was not dead but may have wished he were.

The party continued, with each of the lubricated pilots taking turns holding "Omar," playfully named after their boss, as he came back to island temperature. In the weeks ahead, we often saw Omar scaling the walls. We noticed he stayed away from the ice machine after that experience, however.

Omar in the days after his big chill

CHAPTER 37

—— ❧ ——

The Homeless Golfer and the Real Estate Offices (Cal)

THE REAL ESTATE offices seemed a likely source of clients. People moving to the island would be looking for a great place to house hunt from. The nice thing about the Pink Fancy was that it was right in Christiansted, where guests could walk easily down to the boardwalk to sample the several excellent restaurants and get a feel for the town. It was only the occasional suburban American guest who found it scary to walk by a couple of homeless-looking Rastas in the dark. These guys were just interesting characters and never actually bothered anyone. We often left our car unlocked on the street. Nothing would be messed with.

One Thursday morning, as I was waiting for my new friend, Hugh, who was Mary's husband, to pick me up for his weekly round of golf, Sebastian, who we believed slept in a tree around the corner, came slowly up Prince Street and spotted my Titleist golf bag. He may have had sandals on or not, pants that had ratted out several years ago, a wifebeater T-shirt with a faint image of a Black

Power fist still visible. Dreadlocks cropped up on his head and hung down to his bare midriff.

"I play golf," Sebastian said in the most unlikely statement I had heard since arriving in paradise. It was one of the great humorous moments of the month, making the "don't judge a book by its cover" axiom true once again. I had some fun talking up Sebastian, and it was clear it had been a while since his golfing days, but he was not perturbed that he wasn't getting to play a lot lately. He just couldn't find the time…or his clubs, maybe.

I visited all the real estate offices, along with every other business in the locale. One thing is for sure in sales and marketing—if you sit at home and hope that business finds you, disappointment is the only outcome you can expect.

One encounter at a particular real estate office got a bit tense before it became a classic opportunity to punch back. As I entered, the agent on duty was not a nicely dressed, middle-aged woman who, after raising the family had found a later-in-life career and become self-sufficient as a real estate agent. That seemed the typical profile, especially on the island. Usually those ladies, like many visitors to the island, had arrived fresh from some sort of loss in their lives. It was frequently a bad divorce, but it could be a narrow escape from the law or the aftermath of the worst possible pain: the loss of a child. We met them all as the occasional guest found us at the Pink.

In this case, the lady at reception was a large, body-builder kind of guy—Bart—who would have looked more at home in a biker bar for fifty-somethings. He appeared ready to rumble at the slightest hint of a liberal invading his right to the Pabst Blue Ribbon he was pounding while arguing about whether we should nuke Baghdad or resort to Agent Orange like he got sprayed with in 'Nam in '68.

He looked at me skeptically as I came in to introduce myself and push the Pink Fancy as the place all their incoming clients would love to be. He was not interested even before he knew what I had come in for. "I am Cal Coolidge," I said. "We recently bought the Pink Fancy up the street." I extended my arm to shake hands.

Bart was having no part of it and snapped back, "That's a gay hotel."

"No, actually, it is not. My wife and I—" I tried to continue with my two-minute elevator speech.

"It's a gay hotel." Bart was not confused.

"Well, Bart, it has actually never been a gay hotel. We did buy it from two lesbians, but it has always been no different than any of the other fine hotels in Christiansted."

"It's a gay hotel," Bart insisted, and clearly, he had dismissed me twenty seconds into the pitch.

Never one to be deterred, I went quickly on to the punch line, asking the highly receptive Bart if he had clients coming in from the mainland who would be looking for temporary lodging.

Bart was not the guy who would make my day. "It's a gay hotel," Bart repeated, not looking like a man who respected anyone's choice of lifestyle. There would be no sale here today.

I couldn't resist saying as I turned to leave, "So, Bart, you seem so sure that it's gay. I'm thinking that certainty could only come from personal experience. How was your stay?"

I ran the four blocks back home.

CHAPTER 38

Hurricane Season (Cal)

OCTOBER ARRIVED, BUT it failed to bring any cooler air in with it. We learned not to expect that until hurricane season officially ended and the Christmas winds blew in. That could happen any time after Thanksgiving, legend had it. Until then, "sweltering" would be these Yankees' description of every day.

The 2006 hurricane season just never developed in the tropics, thankfully.

A small scare cropped up on Columbus Day weekend. The forecast called for heavy rains as a tropical depression made its way up the windward islands, hitting Montserrat, Saint Lucia, Barbados, and their neighbors. We could expect hard rains on Sunday night. Wind did not appear to be a problem with this storm, just water. I breathed a sigh of relief, knowing that informing the few guests we had that we did not have a working generator would not be fun. If high winds had been forecasted, I might have faced another $3,000 day at the hardware store in Gallows Bay, buying a new generator to go with the burned-up one on repair back order that was due to return in January.

Cal Coolidge and Joan Coolidge

The tin roof on the schoolhouse building where Joan and I spent our seven hours a night in air conditioning started singing at about 11:00 p.m. This was not rain; this was a deluge. The rat-a-tat of large droplets went from what most people would call heavy rain to the sound of fifteen assault rifles opening up at once. The roar of a waterfall was so loud that both Joan and I sat upright in bed under the constantly spinning ceiling fans. The power was still on, praise the Lord. We guessed it had been raining for an hour before the major deluge set in. We thought it would be over in twenty minutes, as most thunderstorms we'd experienced in Virginia were.

We, however, were now experiencing a tropical storm that was packed with moisture from the southern Atlantic. After four hours, we thought we might be under the southern Atlantic. I put my feet down from the bed onto the bricks that normally provided them a cool sensation as I headed to the bathroom. Tonight, they were not cool; they were submerged! We had so much water rushing by the schoolhouse cottage that it had totally saturated the ground below and was finding its way up through the masonry. A pipe hadn't broken—we were actually floating as groundwater seeped up through the mortar between the bricks. This meant a lot of things were getting wet.

That kicked off a twenty-eight-hour period in which Joan and I did nothing but battle water. We quickly did our best to visit every room, getting anything we could off the floor. The lower-level rooms were seeping groundwater, as had the schoolhouse building. The canopy that protected the breakfast-bar area was sagging under the weight of hundreds of pounds of Caribbean water. We quickly devised a broom tool we could push up from underneath to get the water over the edge with a huge splash onto the Spanish tile around the pool. The pool was already full to overflowing, and water was looking for escape routes.

Using two large, flat brooms, we pushed water down the seventeen steps of stone and onto the street below. Water went down them much easier and faster than I could come up hauling guests' luggage or liquids from PayLow. By noontime, the street was rushing water at least a foot deep. Stones a foot in diameter were tumbling in the current, and, of course, idiots were trying to drive through it. Every twenty minutes, it seemed that the canopy had refilled, and the process began all over again.

Before the roads became impassable, I made a trip to the hardware store and purchased a water vacuum. The vacuum and I worked nonstop for four hours, keeping the seeping water at bay. Two hours later, it was time to start over again.

A rain gauge wouldn't have helped us estimate the total rainfall. You could not have emptied it fast enough or often enough. My best guess was that about thirty-one inches had fallen in twenty-eight hours. I had a steel milk pail sitting on the first deck that was fourteen inches high, and I had emptied it twice. Both times, it was already totally overflowing.

We wouldn't have to worry about the cisterns for a while...and we had survived with no permanent damage. Joan and I were beyond exhausted. We had moved the two guests we had at that time to our highest ground. They barely dared come out of the room for a day and a half but were nice enough to offer to help. We asked them to just stay dry.

October had come to an end. The heat continued, the guests were few, and every week was a combination of discovering how I would spend a grand fixing yet another thing and continuing to build a client base for "high season," if not before that.

PART 4

The Exit

CHAPTER 39

Light at the End of the Tunnel? (Cal)

IT MAY HAVE been at about this point that Mary revealed that although she had only had the listing for the Pink Fancy for about six months when we came along, it had actually been listed for sale for a least a year with another agency and broker. She also thought it had been unofficially on the market for perhaps two years prior to that.

The hotel phone rang. Before I could get out the standard greeting that was designed to make the potential tourist think she'd just found her way to paradise and the great luck to book the last available room, Mary said, "Cal, I was in the shower this morning, and what you asked me to think about hit me! I now recall that there was a couple who tried very hard to buy the hotel about a year and a half ago. Something went wrong during the deal, I heard, and they ended up buying a small place on the edge of Christiansted." Mary explained that they had been clients of a very active agent on the island who had a reputation for being aggressive.

"We need to find those people, Mary," I directed, my optimistic mind already wondering how much they'd offered during the deal that had blown up. Could we be saved?

Mary was to contact the mystery agent to see if any interest was still there, and I thought that immediately, if not sooner, was the time to do that. This would be the first that anyone outside the trusted circle would know that we were serious about selling the recently acquired hotel. Having the word on the street that your hotel was for sale could be damaging, as competitors talked to tourists. You certainly didn't want a "For Sale" sign hanging out front just below the "Vacancy" notice. But if the object was to get it sold, you had to show your hand, didn't you?

Apparently, aggressive agents return calls quickly. Mary called back that afternoon with good news and bad news. The bad news was that Tabby (short for Samantha) had no intention of telling Mary or us anything about these people unless we had signed a listing agreement, which was understandable. They were her clients, and a split 10 percent commission on a million-dollar-plus sale gets attention, especially if they were still interested. She could likely facilitate a sale with virtually no marketing investment by the agents. The good news was, Tabby had called them, and her first report was that they were thrilled to hear the property might be available again and were very interested. Wow, was that tidbit an amazing ray of sunlight.

After learning what we could about the potential buyers, which was not much, we signed a listing agreement with the stipulation that no visible marketing of the hotel sale would take place until this buyer had a chance to make an offer. The list price was agreed to be exactly what the closing price had been five months earlier: $1,195,000.

CHAPTER 40

— ✤ —

So, Where Is This Offer? (Cal)

ALTHOUGH WE HAD no credible way of verifying what had happened when the first deal these people had cut with Dora and Spike fell apart, we had our ears open and probed a few sources who might know something. We heard that the couple was from Raleigh-Durham, North Carolina, apparently well heeled, and in the commercial real estate business. We weren't surprised to hear rumors that the negotiation had become a pissing contest with the "gals," and the buyers had walked. The best rumor I'd picked up was that there had been an offer somewhat over $1,000,000.

Without a buyer in sight prior to this development, I had mentally pondered what I might accept in order to extract us from this mess. The number was scary to think about; we had to get enough to pay off the note, but anything over that would be gravy. I had days when I would have accepted just a smell of that gravy. It would be painful, but it would be behind us.

I did all I could not to call Mary daily. When I did resist, I'd find myself walking by her office and just stopping in to say hi. "They are working on it" lasted for a couple of weeks. Then it became "Next Friday, they have a property that is going to close, and they plan to make an offer after that."

Next Friday came and went: "The property didn't close."

Realistically, we had no right to feel anxious or deserving of a timely offer, but when you are an optimist, you just can't understand why the world doesn't run on your schedule.

Needing to get away from the hotel on a Sunday afternoon in late October, I made my way down the boardwalk and joined a sparse crew of locals who were watching the Washington Redskins play the New York Giants in a very boring six-six tie. The old-school pre-HD TV that hung over the open-air bar at Styxx was barely visible with the amount of midday sunlight that reflected off the water just behind where I sat. Across the bar were three refugees from the mainland who had likely shown up to do carpentry or unlicensed electrical work after Hurricane Hugo had leveled the island in 1989. Some who had done that never left, scraping out an unglamorous existence. To hear that any of these guys had had dental work done in a decade would have been a shock. They had probably seven teeth between them.

Things were hitting a low for me. Here I was, just four years removed from an executive lifestyle that had included first-class flights and thousand-dollar suits, not to mention the occasional corporate-jet ride. I looked at the toothless guys. Was that going to be me in five years? Would not having health insurance while losing ten grand a month in low season make it so bad that Joan would not get the annual scans she required after breast cancer? Would I wear out my already-hurting, fifty-five-year-old left knee on those freakin' seventeen steps of stone, hauling up mass quantities of liquids? Would I then have no way of getting it repaired? Not to mention dental work—that was not easy even to *find* on the island, never mind pay for. Jesus, you needed to think about this before you went all in on the Caribbean lifestyle.

I'd been part of the leadership teams of two major electronics firms that each did over $2 billion in annual sales. I'd been on the short list of industry executives who made golf trips to Pine Valley, Pebble Beach, Cyprus Point, and Saint Andrews. I'd probably attended two hundred black-tie events in the Washington arena and hobnobbed with the rich and powerful. I had called it "life on scholarship."

Look at me now, mixing it up with a bunch of bohemians who had somehow come up with the funds to buy today's eight beers and tomorrow's fish sandwich, but that was all.

I actually loved meeting these island characters, and in a way, they had a life that many who were playing the corporate game might actually have been willing to trade for (providing that they were the ones lying on beach chairs, not fetching towels and drinks). But this was as depressing a day as one could imagine. How much further could I fall and survive—and was I about to take Joan with me?

I couldn't bring myself to stay for the end of the football game. I had to get back to where Joan could keep me away from sharp objects.

CHAPTER 41

—— ⌀ ——

Turning Point—
the Call (Cal)

As I MADE the walk back down the deserted boardwalk toward the hotel, a Seaborne Airlines craft was, apparently as a result of the wind shifting slightly from the north, making an unusual approach that was going to clear the faded pink roof of the Pink Fancy by less than a hundred feet. It was exciting to be sitting around the pool when one of the Twin Otter aircraft swooped by that close. Today, my depressed mind couldn't help but fantasize about a fiery crash directly into the property I was becoming convinced was unsellable. It would have solved my problem…but that thinking was just wrong. How does that kind of tragic-ending solution even enter your mind? I was not proud of allowing myself to go that low.

As I passed the Seaborne terminal, I stopped to engage for a minute with the usual small group of cab drivers who killed time awaiting the next flight by sitting around a low table on three discarded folding chairs and one wooden fruit crate, playing dominos. The island chatter was constant among the group. My favorite,

Jacobs, was part of it today. Jacobs had the voice of God. James Earl Jones might be an apt comparison. I liked Jacobs: his perfect diction and the king's English that came out of his happy face were soothing.

My state of depression was evident to him. "How is my lord and innkeeper to the world doing today?" Jacobs boomed in that rich, baritone voice.

"You fellas are going to teach me to play one day soon, aren't you?" I responded.

"Any day, my man, any day."

In the remaining two hundred steps, I would pass by Sebastian, the "homeless golfer." I heard him rustling under the mango tree that apparently served as his home, his hammock hanging between two branches. Sebastian was smiling. He had no worries.

I passed the small market that could find a way to exchange food stamps for alcohol and tobacco products and the barbershop-laundromat that sat across Prince Street from the hotel. None of the inhabitants were spending their Sunday afternoon in the state of depression that I had worked myself into.

As I unlocked and came through the gate at the bottom of the seventeen steps of stone, Sally and Peanut ran down to greet me with unconditional affection. They may have sensed my depression, but their only mission was to wag their tails silly and say, "Welcome back, Dad." Most loved dogs have one mission—giving love back. On this day, I didn't deserve that love, but they were offering it.

Cal Coolidge and Joan Coolidge

Joan heard the gate close below and could see on the security camera that I had returned, hopefully in a better mood than when I'd left. "I was just starting to call you. You need to call Mary. She needs to tell you about a call she just got—something about providing comps to another agent."

I hit speed-dial three on my cell as I trudged up the seventeen steps of stone, my own weight on this day compounded by that of the world on my shoulders from my depression. Mary's mobile phone was usually the best way to reach her. "Your call cannot be placed at this time," stated the recording that often plagued the island's cell network.

"Did she say where she was?" I asked Joan, who wasn't sure. At four o'clock on an October Sunday afternoon, it was unlikely that Mary was in the office, but I would try her there next.

Mary answered, apparently at her desk. She had known it was me. "Cal, I received a call about a half hour ago from Shelly, who is an agent for Sunshine Properties." I knew they specialized in beachfront property but little else. "She has a couple from New Jersey who are looking seriously at the Palms at Pelican Cove, the eight-room place I showed you and Joan in February. She called wanting a comp from the Pink Fancy. They are about to make an offer there and want to know what the sale price was. Are you OK if I tell them? They'd be able to get it on Monday at the island-records building."

"Have you told them that we are for sale?" I responded.

"Not yet. I wanted to check with you before I revealed that. You know we were to give Tabby a chance with the Werths before we went public."

"I'd say forty days is plenty of time, wouldn't you? We need to get those people over here. You know the Pink Fancy will outshine the Palms any day, Mary. Call them, and invite them over. I'm OK with telling them we are for sale, what our closing price was, and, hell, give them all the info they need—but tell them they need to see the Pink before they make any offer. Once they get here, I'll handle the tour. Just get them to come over. Cocktails await."

Joan scrambled to mix up the daily brew; Mary called back to say that the prospects were on their way, and she'd be along to help out.

The threesome of Shelly, Woody, and Alice arrived just after Mary came up those seventeen steps of stone.

Woody was in his upper thirties, pleasant, and in high gear. Alice, his red-haired wife, seemed a bit more reserved. She seemed to be humoring Woody in his quest; she had an Irish accent. We quickly learned that they worked in the Poconos and that she had hotel experience. Woody had sales experience, but it wasn't clear in what field. I had cast away my state of deep depression from an hour ago and was at my best as the "people guy" who knew how to bond with customers. Joan hadn't seen much of that out of me in months.

After pleasantries, the tour of the grounds was underway. I was doing my best not to oversell. I somehow sensed that Woody would respond best to a realistic soft sell. The entire property showed well. We got into nine of the unoccupied rooms with everyone in tow. When the tour headed to the utility room-cum-electrical-pump room, the ladies had had enough. They retreated poolside under the canopy. Joan whipped out the pitcher of our special Pink Fancy cocktails.

Getting Woody's story wasn't hard; it appeared that they were determined to cast away the "back-home" life, and they knew they could make it on the island if they found the right property. I was spending equal amounts of time telling Woody about the island, the hotel, and the business, and probing him, trying my best to qualify the couple. Could they pull off buying a million-plus property? Where was the money coming from? Did they have a good sense of what they'd be getting into?

Unfortunately, my sense was that it would be a real stretch for them. I knew I'd been naïve and had let making the deal and the excitement of it all make me think everything would be easy. I knew better now, and although I would have loved to move this property into someone else's hands, I saw trouble ahead for this couple unless they were in a better financial position than was apparently the case.

While still doing my best to show the hotel well, I was being totally forthcoming and honest with Woody about how hard the business was. Maybe Woody had never worked with someone who was an underselling master, but he was not to be deterred.

The two real estate agents recognized that Woody was becoming more interested every time I threw up a caution flag. They didn't know how this was happening, but they knew to let it brew. All four ladies visited with one another as the tour and discussion of all things Pink Fancy went on between Woody and me.

Daylight was fading; Woody and Alice must have been exhausted after getting themselves ready to buy one Caribbean property in the morning and then finding an even better option this afternoon. They were leaving for home Monday, so "we'd hear from them." That didn't seem likely once they came to their senses.

CHAPTER 42

Monday Morning (Cal)

IT WAS MARY again. "Shelly is asking if Woody and Alice could come back again before they head for their flight."

Just before eleven, our new friends from New Jersey arrived. Shelly must have picked them up and was going to take them directly to the airport after this second visit to us. Woody had a thousand questions. He also had some ideas of how he'd change this or that on the property and in the positioning of the hotel with clients. He must not have slept a wink last night. He was full of ideas, and I liked all of them.

I asked him directly about how he was planning to put together the cash to buy a property like this or the Palms at Pelican Shores. It wasn't clear that he had so many good ideas on that front. He'd talk with the banks on the island; they'd be receptive. I didn't offer an opinion on that but suggested he might want to secure some private investors if he was serious.

I had qualified clients prior to opening brokerage accounts for them and prior to selling them insurance. I knew how to probe and was pretty good at assessing a client's net worth after an hour of chitchat. Woody was coming through as doing OK but not as someone sitting on the required assets it would take to pull this deal off—if he did make an offer.

With that in mind, I continued to throw out red flags to Woody, and Woody kept offering rationales of how he could handle everything.

Another nearly two hours of looking over the property went fast, and they were headed for the flight home. We'd hear from them, Woody promised.

Woody and Alice were prospects—well, maybe suspects—but nothing that came across after three and a half hours of touring and talking had given any of us remaining on the island a huge boost of confidence that they were qualified prospects who could pull it off.

Most likely, the excitement would die down once they got home and into their normal routine. Even the former world-class optimist couldn't see this going further. At best, maybe word would get back to the North Carolina people that someone was showing interest. I suggested to Mary that the rumor should circulate in the Saint Croix real estate community.

Monday and Tuesday passed with normal hotel business, which meant nearly no business. Wednesday, the phone rang; it was Woody with lots more questions and lots more probing by both him and me. He wasn't bothering to go through his agent with questions; I had said to call anytime, and he was. The agents were a little miffed, but they saw the two of us bonding and said, "Have at it."

He'd somehow found interest with Lord knows who providing some cash, and they thought they could sell their house and generate a bit of capital. I remained doubtful. I was beginning to give Woody stronger warnings about the business. "Be careful to think this through" was my advice. I was becoming worried that I might escape the island but leave my new, underfunded friend in a failing position. I'd sure feel better if someone with deeper pockets came along.

On Friday, just five days after I hit the bottom of my emotional depression, Mary called. "We have an offer."

"Really?" I said in a hopeful voice. "Tell me more: From whom, and how much?"

"It's from Woody, and they are offering $895,000 versus our asking price of $1,195,000. Cal, there are quite a few conditions, including them finding financing locally on the island. But it is an offer."

The weight on my chest was lighter; there was an offer. Maybe not a good one and maybe not from the most qualified buyer, but it was an offer. It was enough to pay off the note to Hank and lose only about a half million. When you have dipped as low as I had allowed myself to go, losing a half million was not the end of the world. Maybe this could work.

"Mary, you need to get word to Tabby that we have an offer. Tell her that her clients are about to lose out on the Pink Fancy for the second time. She doesn't need to know any other details, just that we have an offer, and it's time for her deep-pocketed clients to step up," I calmly said before even commenting on the offer at hand. "Tell her we have forty-eight hours to respond; we want to give her people a chance."

Mary may have been a little shocked; she had seen the emotional stress I had put myself under. I had an offer—wasn't I even going to counter it? These offers didn't come along every day on Saint Croix. Was I crazy?

I related the exchange to Joan when I got back to the hotel; she walked away in disbelief. "You aren't even going to counter? You are an asshole."

"I really worry about Woody actually pulling this off, and if he does, I can't see them succeeding."

"Do we care about that?"

"Well, I care about them being able to close, and yes, I don't feel good about them getting into the same shit we are in. We've got forty-eight hours to respond. Let's see what happens."

CHAPTER 43

꘎

Thursday (Cal)

WE REALLY NEEDED to make a counteroffer on Wednesday per the contract presented, but then again, this was the island. Things worked on a little different schedule. We'd hold off and let Mary make some excuse for us.

At 4:30 p.m Thursday., just after we'd sweated out one more day of cleaning, laundry, and mold scrubbing, Mary called. "We have an offer from Tabby's people."

This offer was better—$1,050,000—and it was cash. There were a few conditions, but it was generally a clean contract. Now we were talking. We'd counter this one, but we'd proceed as if the sale wasn't the most important thing in our lives, even though nothing else had come close—at least from a financial perspective, not to mention from a sanity perspective.

Friday afternoon, I met with Mary. "Let's make a counteroffer at $1,180,000. We'll show a little movement, but it will indicate that we are not running a fire sale." Mary was skeptical but helped develop the counteroffer and got it back to Tabby. The buyers were in the commercial real estate business; they weren't naïve, and hopefully they wouldn't walk just because we'd barely budged.

But hey! The asking price was fair. We were going to stick with that premise.

Wednesday, a fax arrived. The new offer was $1,095,000: they'd moved $45,000, and we were still just $15,000 below our break-even point. It would be nice to get another move out of them prior to proposing a split; we could live with that.

We moved our counteroffer to $1,175,000, just a $5,000 drop, trying to signal that we were close to our bottom price. The rest of Thursday was quiet. We were surprised that Shelly hadn't demanded an answer to the offer from her clients. Somehow, Mary must have quelled her inquiries. We wondered why Woody hadn't called me directly—maybe he was coming to his senses.

On Friday morning, Mary advised that Tabby wanted to meet with us. She'd had a message from her clients. Could she come over at one? I suspected the message wasn't that her client was seeing things our way.

I had made plans to spend the day with old friends from Connecticut who were on property for the week. They'd be leaving Sunday. Maybe then would be a good time to meet. Tabby responded sharply that it had to be before noon on Saturday, or her clients were going to walk. OK, how about eleven on Saturday? She could be a bit aggressive, and I was certain I was under her skin.

The meeting convened alongside our small residence on a perfectly delightful shaded patio. Tabby arrived in power-real estate attire—what you might expect in New York or Dallas. Spiked heels and as close to a business suit as I had seen on the island. She was playing the power card. Joan and I cleaned up for the meeting, but it was T-shirts and sandals for us. Mary, always tasteful in her appearance, was going to play arbitrator here, we could tell.

It took only a few opening lines from Tabby about our uncooperative counteroffers, our inexperience with the island market, and how fortunate we were to be dealing with her well-heeled clients to make Joan see red. It was a silent red, but I could see it. She did not like this woman.

I knew Tabby was correct on all three statements, but I had thought out my strategy for today. They were at $1,095,000 now. My intelligence on their previous offer to the last owners that had fallen through told me that it was rumored to be $1,100,000. I had already decided that if I could get her to raise their bid to $1,100,000 or more, I was going to accept. Yes, it would be a tough loss of about $100,000, and more once we paid the agents, but it wasn't a half a million, and we'd get back home with cash in our pockets.

"Tabby, I know we are a long way apart. I'm hoping we can find common ground. If you could get your clients to give us another offer over $1,100,000, I think I can find a way to compromise. Have they given you authority to do that? I'm asking you to make a move of $5,000. If you do, I believe you'll be happy with my counter."

Her response was vicious. "Mr. Coolidge, we have a fair offer on the table. My clients have the wherewithal to pay cash on that offer. You can take it or leave it."

I was cool when I responded after a long pause: "Well, Tabby, you might be right, but I think that before I take it, I owe it to Joan and myself to reengage with the first offer we received last week. We'll do that today and get back to you by Monday."

I had called Tabby's bluff, and she was pissed. She could have cut the deal right there on the spot for $5,000, but she'd taken the aggressive route. We'd see how this played out.

Tabby, in a huff, left Joan and me with Mary. Joan was proud of me for the first time in months; she'd really not cared for Tabby's style. Mary was smiling; perhaps no one had ever stood up to the overly aggressive Tabby before. She wasn't going to comment on the exchange, but she had clearly been entertained.

Mary was tasked with contacting Shelly at Sunshine Properties. I instructed her to tell the clients that we were in negotiation with Tabby's clients and what our last offer to them had been. If they wanted to make us another offer, we said, please do. But we asked her not to tell them anything else.

CHAPTER 44

— ✎ —

Meanwhile, Back at the Hotel (Cal)

SOON AFTER WE had implemented our consultants' instructions back in August, the work we'd done getting the property listed through TripAdvisor, Hotels.com, and other online-booking sites did in fact yield the occasional booking, and the efforts we'd made with the local businesses were paying off, however slowly. We had seen occupancy creep up as colder weather in the north started to show its head; unfortunately, it was a warm fall, and the long-term forecast was for an easy winter up north.

We gleefully found that a high school friend of mine from Connecticut had booked a week: November 5 through 12. Alan and his wife, Diane, had kept in loose touch with me over thirty-five-plus years. Alan had been a partner of mine in the usual high school pranks and sports; having them visit for a week was greatly appreciated and did wonders for my attitude. But it also coincided with the pressure of this negotiation.

When I picked Diane and Alan up at the airport, I took them back into town and the hotel via the scenic route along the north shore, up over the Beast, and along the crashing waves of Cane Bay. I had time to confide in them that a lot was going on.

The offer had been received from Woody and Alice a few days before my friends arrived. I informed them of our struggles, and I asked them that if we seemed distracted to please forgive us. They were gracious and undemanding guests.

Once again, we were having a week of "living the life," sharing Pink Fancy cocktails on the upper deck, watching the almost daily rainbows appear as the scattered showers developed between Saint Croix and the other US Virgin Islands of Saint Thomas and Saint John. Alan treated us to dinner almost every night—if in return we'd share the secrets of the secluded spots and entertain them with stories of this island life.

Alan and I made an afternoon trip to Cane Bay to take a scuba-diving lesson the afternoon of the showdown with Tabby, a first-time experience for both of us. Reaching depths of forty feet, we glided through the colorful fish, saw a large barracuda, and ventured out over the wall. The experience of looking down into the depths of blackness was scary but stimulating. Life was good, at least for this week, among friends. Never mind that I simultaneously had a wild negotiation ongoing; I excelled at compartmentalizing things in my life.

All good things come to an end. Sunday, I drove my friends back to the airport for the afternoon flight to Miami connecting to Hartford. It was a particularly warm November day. As I left the airport, I found the cheapest spot to fill up the Escape. As I pumped gas in the bright sun, my cell rang. It was Joan. "Cal, Mary just called. Woody has made us another offer."

"Really? How much is it?"

"Cal, it is $20,000 over our last offer. It is $1,195,000."

CHAPTER 45

Calling for Best and Finals (Cal)

Whoa, what was happening here? The loss we had been prepared to take had just gone from close to $200,000 to back to damn near breakeven after paying our closing costs. Woody had stepped up big-time. There was nothing new, however, in my apprehension about his ability to actually close, not to mention my concern that he and Alice were getting themselves in over their heads with a project that might be doomed to failure without deeper pockets than he had, at least as they looked on the surface.

There was still another active bid on the table, but now it was $100,000 short. On the other hand, those bidders had been reported to be well qualified and offering cash. A sure thing, if there was one, when it came to getting a successful closing.

Oh my God, I had come within a whisker of getting another $5,000 out of Tabby and settling for $1,100,000 on Saturday, but she'd played hardball. Here we were on Sunday afternoon, looking at another $95,000. But would it happen?

I went directly to Mary's office on the return trip to the hotel; I found her holding Woody's bid. It did still have a condition that they had to get financing, but Mary had been assured verbally that they had relatives or friends who were volunteering to be the bank.

"Mary, let both parties know their best and final offer is due here Monday at noon. We are going to take the best offer and end this thing." It wasn't clear she'd had many cases like this: a seller who, a week earlier, might have given the place away and with no offers on the table to now having two bids and a seller who was acting like he did this every day.

CHAPTER 46

— ❧ —

Another Monday Morning... Another Bluff (Cal)

AT 10:30 A.M. Monday, Mary called the hotel. I was doing something on the lower level, such as cleaning toilets and finding more hair under beds. Joan took Mary's call. Woody had submitted a new offer another $10,000 higher, but Mary needed to talk to me about Tabby's client. Joan brought the phone to me. "It seems that our North Carolina prospect will make another offer, but he will only do it over the phone," Mary reported.

"What the hell? Everyone knows we need it in writing. That is crazy!" I protested.

"Well, that is what they are telling us. He will only do it over the phone. Please come down to my office. We should hear what he has to say."

"So I am supposed to compare a verbal offer to one I have in writing?"

"Please just come here, and we'll listen to what he has to say."

What bullshit, I thought as I hung up. Should I call her back and tell her to let them know we were going with the written offer from Woody? I got out of my sweated-out

T-shirt, showered, and headed into town, torn as to how I should act when this prima donna tried to change the rules of the negotiation. I was beginning to like Woody's written offer better all the time.

When I walked in, Mary was on the line with Tabby on speaker. Tabby was in her familiar mode of hard-ass when I joined the conversation. "Rock wants to talk with you prior to making his offer. You have to allow him that."

"I do? What is it about having an offer here by noon, in writing, that he doesn't understand?"

"Rock is an important man. He buys and sells commercial properties every week. He isn't going to have you force him to keep bidding every day. He doesn't do auctions!"

"This is not an auction. He just needs to get his best and final offer here, and I will treat it like that…best and final." Tabby and I were not bonding.

Tabby abruptly announced that she'd patched in the team in Raleigh-Durham and introduced Rock over the phone. He launched into his arrogant spiel before I could get a word in edgewise, and over speakerphone, it was impossible to break into the conversation, which went something like this: "Mr. Coolidge, you seem to think you have me over a barrel, but you do not. I am going to make you a revised offer, but I have one rule. You must say yes or no while I am on the phone. Otherwise, I am not going bother with it."

Finally, a moment of silence, giving me time to break in. "Listen, Mr. Werth, I laid out the rules on Sunday.

You and the other bidder were to submit offers in writing by noon today, and I plan to take the better of the two. What is so hard about that? I planned to compare the two offers, discuss them with my wife, and—"

The momentary pause allowed him to cut in again. "I thought I was dealing with someone who could make a decision. Why do you have to talk to your wife? Aren't you the decision maker?" Rock said in a very pompous, wiseass tone.

I was not liking this exchange, but I wasn't going to take the bait. "Listen, Mr. Werth, I am not going to ask you for another offer, and I think you know I will need it in writing. That is all I asked, and I asked Mary to inform both parties that I plan to accept whichever is higher. You have to respect that."

"I don't have to respect anything. You have my condition. Take it or leave it!"

This guy was being a prick and trying to pull the power to his side of the table. I had been down this road before and was doing my best to stay levelheaded. I felt like I should send this punk to sit in the corner until he agreed to play better with others.

Mary, across the desk, was staying out of this testosterone battle that was brewing in a three-way conference call. I asked for a minute to caucus in her conference room, away from the speaker that connected the parties.

"Mary, he is being a jerk. How can I take his offer verbally? Does he think we are bluffing him about the other offer or something? Well, we aren't, are we? We have Woody's offer in writing. What was it again?"

Woody had raised it $10,000 to $1,205,000. We were now over our asking price before we paid agents and closing costs. Yet my concern over him actually being able to pull it off remained.

Mary was letting me mull it over and would likely be supportive of whatever I concluded.

"Well, I guess we may as well hear the offer."

CHAPTER 47

—— ❧ ——

The Offer (Cal)

"OK, Rock, I'll listen to your offer. But tell me, am I to assume that all of the conditions in your last written offer are still in effect?"

He might have not taken time to consider that, but he quickly said, "Yes. And, as I said, you have to say yes or no while I am on the phone. Our offer is $1,206,000."

What a freakin' coincidence.

I looked across the desk at Mary. She wasn't acknowledging anything, and maybe there was nothing to acknowledge, but I could not help but think there were no secrets on the island. "Mary, can we caucus again in the conference room?" We left the line open.

I asked for the former written offer and confirmed that the Werths' offer had included not just the hotel, but the vehicle we had purchased for $13,000. Woody's offer was silent about the vehicle. The last thing I wanted on the day we were leaving for home was to sell a vehicle, so it didn't matter that much, but I had said I was going to take the better of the two offers. Despite all the concerns I had about Woody's ability to close, Rock had been such a prick that I was having trouble overlooking that $12,000 difference.

Mary and I walked back to the speakerphone that had been open now for more than two hours. I said as calmly as I could with this much adrenaline running, "If I have to say yes or no while you are on the phone...the answer is no."

The silence in the office was absolute. The party at the other end had not seen that coming. After about fifteen seconds that seemed like two minutes, Tabby piped up, "Well, there is always a winner and a loser in these things." *Click*. They were gone.

Mary and I looked at each other. Had our best opportunity just been kicked out the door?

CHAPTER 48

— ✆ —

Down to One (Cal)

"WE BETTER LOOK at Woody's contract, I guess. Geez Louise, this is wearing me out," I muttered while wondering how it would end. Would Woody actually pull this off, or would we waste a couple of months trying to get him to the closing and then find out the whole deal had blown up?

The faxed contract had, in fact, removed the condition that they had to secure local financing. There were a few items that we'd have to clarify, since it called for all property, both personal and what was part of the hotel, to remain on-site after closing. Surely Woody and Alice weren't trying to lay claim to our personal belongings, which included my golf clubs and Joan's jewelry.

Mary put a call in to Shelly, the agent representing Woody and Alice. She was off island, having departed in the midst of this for a getaway to Florida. We left her a message asking her to call immediately. We didn't have a number to contact Woody directly. This was a problem.

Mary and I went to work on the contract offer, accepting everything that made sense and removing the references to personal property. The offer of $1,205,000 would be accepted in the clean contract offer we were creating. The counteroffer sheet came into being over the next forty-five minutes. "I'd feel a lot better if we had a way to reach Woody with the news that he was the last man standing."

Mary's cell phone rang. "I better answer this. It looks like Tabby's number."

"Is there a way we could get back into this?" asked Tabby. Mary had hit speaker before she answered. She looked across the desk at me without saying anything, wondering what I would say. Tabby was back on her very high heels.

I was thinking, *Tabby, you must not be real popular in Raleigh, North Carolina, right now. Three days ago, you could have closed this deal for just another $5,000, and now you are begging to get back in for an extra $100,000 of your client's money.* I was smiling but held back the thought.

"Tabby," I said, "you get the Werths' offer to us in writing within the next hour, and we'll consider it...and, by the way, we're not including the vehicle at that price."

"I will have attorney Byron Rutkies's office bring it to you; it will be there by one o'clock. My clients want this property." *Click.*

"Mary, I'm buying lunch. Let's go. We are back to two bidders. Something tells me that Mrs. Werth put nighttime into play when the arrogant SOB informed her that he'd blown the deal for the second time."

The fresh offer arrived while Mary and I were still enjoying tacos on the mango-tree plaza nearby. Mary's partner walked it over to us and sat down. The offer price was the same, the vehicle was specifically not included, and the terms and conditions were beyond fair. The buyers were aware that we had a group of friends coming in early January; they wanted to close as early as January 3, but we could stay to enjoy the time with our friends and receive the revenue from their visit. That was thoughtful.

The only new item was that they planned to send a manager from North Carolina to run the place, and we were to offer him training between December 26 through closing. That was easily accepted, providing he was willing to work alongside both of us as we did the daily work. I wondered how he'd enjoy the toilet cleaning and mold patrol that were the less glamorous parts of small-hotel management.

The deal was a total cash offer, and we were assured that the funds were available. We'd be foolish not to accept all this from a qualified buyer. We signed the offer and returned it in thirty minutes. Woody and Alice would never know how close they came to getting themselves in over their heads.

The day had become one that we'd remember forever. The walk back to the Pink Fancy felt like it was on air. One hell of a weight was off my back, and the folks on the boardwalk must have wondered what it was that had turned my attitude around. It would be a few days before rumors got around the village. Virtually no one had even been aware that the Pink Fancy was being sold again.

When word did get out, I was stopped numerous times by other business owners. "How did you do that?

I have had my business for sale for thirteen years, and I have never had an offer" was the most memorable comment. "You had two offers? How the hell did that happen?" "We heard that one of them was really your cousin. Don't tell me you created that bidding war…"

Some probed for evidence that it had all been part of some grand scheme. Why had we moved all that way only to flip the place and head home smiling seven months later? Had something interesting been found on the property? What the hell had it been? Had we known it was there prior to buying the place? Had those money-hungry gals not known they were showering on top of half stack of tax-free bearer bonds? The rumors were out there. Some might have been planted, some were pure fantasy, and some might have had some truth to them.

CHAPTER 49

— ❧ —

Thanksgiving, Christmas, Various Happy Times (Cal)

IT WASN'T HERE yet, but in fact, high season was coming; they hadn't been lying about that. The calls began to roll in, however slowly. January was looking like it could be a decent month.

Ron Milner, the teaching pro at our country club in Mount Vernon, Virginia, had sought a way to keep working with his clients and promoted a trip for some of our Alexandria friends during the second week of January. He schemed to turn it into a winter month for himself away from two young ones under three at home. I was an accomplice.

We heard from an artist who loved to bring her students to the Pink Fancy and Saint Croix. The area around the grounds provided the kind of natural scenes that she loved to teach her lady students to paint. Her group would fill the place in early February. It wouldn't be our sale, but it felt good to be producing activity. We had inherited the hotel, admittedly in low season, with absolutely zero advance bookings. By the time we finally closed on January 17, advance bookings totaled over $100,000, looking out to the end of May 2007.

Maybe the locals had been right. "You need to get through a high season," they had said. Joan and I were happy that things were looking up for the property, but we totally agreed that for us, things *were* really looking up. We'd be on the mainland in a month with virtually everything we'd left with.

With the load off my back, I reverted to my "Mr. Sociable" role and someone actually fun to be around. Once again, I was the overly optimistic extrovert.

In November, we accepted an invitation to join our webmaster and closest advisor on the island, Wendy, and her husband for what was probably our most thankful Thanksgiving ever. Wendy and Bob were committed to seeing Saint Croix thrive. We might have been traitors to them professionally, but they were happy for us. Wendy had seen us struggling. Her GotoStCroix marketing team had done their best to make our time on the island pleasant. She knew how hard it was to be a success on Saint Croix, but she had become the most reliable marketing and positive-information source anyone could find. Her www.gotostcroix.com online campaign and the now-HD webcam gives outsiders a daily view of this wonderful island.

Visitors from Vermont just prior to Christmas were entertaining. Terry was an ultramarathoner at age seventy-plus. He inquired where it would be safe for him to run a mere ten miles before breakfast. I cut a deal with him that if he was ready at sunrise, we'd drive to the deserted south side of the island, and I would ride my bike along the ocean-side road for thirty minutes going east and then return, and he'd do the same running. That activity cleared the mind and got me back to the hotel fully charged to clean six to eight rooms by nine in the morning. As I emerged in the last moments of darkness at 6:15 a.m., I could count on Terry to be silently waiting in a chair, ready to run.

As the holidays approached, we hosted my partner from Smith Barney, who had been covering my clients while our dramedy played out. Jeremy "Big Country" Nichols was approaching thirty and had recently, after a twelve-year courtship of his high-school sweetheart, Cassie, set a date for a June wedding. His dad decided to come along for the trip, thinking that his days of alone time with Jeremy might be coming to an end.

Jeremy "Big County" Nichols and his dad Gary arrive

That visit was full of laughs and rum. A charter fishing trip was a highlight for me, but young Jeremy spent a good portion of the time looking slightly green and rushing to the side of the boat to puke. We did bring home a trove of mahimahi, which grilled up nicely that evening for dinner—fresh fish, to say the least.

The life of the carefree innkeeper wasn't bad—it was getting to that carefree point that was the tough part.

On December 20, we received a call from a woman who was the daughter of Jerry and Mildred Josefson of Staten Island. Her parents had come to visit her on nearby Saint Thomas, where she spent the winters. She had seen an article about us in the *Saint Croix Avis* when we had arrived to begin our adventure.

Her parents were going to be celebrating their fiftieth anniversary in January 2007, and she wanted to know if we were familiar with a small hotel on Saint Croix named the Clover Crest. Her parents had honeymooned there in January 1957. It took a few calls to local historians, but we found the Clover Crest, although it had long ago been closed and overtaken by the jungle.

The visit had inspired the front-page story in the legendary *Saint Croix Avis*, the daily newspaper that chose an inexplicable variety of national stories to run in bold print around the local-interest issues that its staff dug up.

Its sports page was famous for having a huge headline and a full page of AP copy about a Wednesday-night NBA game between, say, Milwaukee and Portland. No one ever explained how they chose these back-page headlines.

The *Avis* sent reporter Tom Eader to the Pink Fancy after being tipped off that an interesting couple with history had arrived. The article read as follows:

❦

TWO VISITS, 50 years

After Honeymoon in 1957, couple celebrates golden anniversary on STX

By Tom Eader

Saint Croix: A New York couple who first visited Saint Croix in 1957 on their honeymoon returned to the big island earlier this week for their second visit to celebrate their 50th anniversary at the Pink Fancy Hotel in Christiansted.

Jerry and Mildred Josefson, got married in Brooklyn NY on January 27, 1957 before flying off to Saint Croix to begin their honeymoon upon the suggestion of a travel agent. They returned this week to celebrate their 50th anniversary.

"I wanted to see how it's changed and remember the good times," Mildred said about returning to Saint Croix for her anniversary.

The Josefsons, while sitting poolside at the Pink Fancy Hotel Thursday during their second visit to Saint Croix, remembered their first trip to the big island almost 50 years ago. Mildred said she and her husband flew to Puerto Rico in order to connect with a smaller aircraft before flying to the tiny tropical island of Saint Croix, secluded in the Caribbean Sea.

"We were honeymooners and young," Mildred recalled. "I was 20 and my husband was 24. We looked like we were running away from home."

During their trip from New York to Saint Croix in 1957, Mildred said she and Jerry were told there would soon be a larger airstrip on Saint Croix to begin accommodating the larger aircraft flying direct from New York and the United States. She said they were told everything was going to become "super modern" on Saint Croix in the future. Fifty years later, air travelers must still fly from the United States to Puerto Rico in order to connect with smaller aircraft before making the jump to Saint Croix since the Henry E. Rohlsen Airport still can't accommodate the larger aircraft.

Nonetheless, the Josefsons arrived on Saint Croix safe and sound in 1957 as they were greeted and picked up from the airport by individuals from the resort they were staying at called the Clover Crest, a hotel that overlooked the sea on the island's west end. Mildred said she was immediately impressed with the island as she referred to it as a "tropical paradise." She said she still feels that way today.

"There are so many spots on Saint Croix that are beautiful, so many vistas overlooking the ocean, I don't know why more people don't come here. It is like a secret."

Back in 1957, Mildred said most of the transportation on the island consisted of donkey and cart. The Josefsons said there was a small number of vehicles on Saint Croix at that time. They said it was, however, difficult to rent a vehicle back then since the demand was greater than the supply. She said individuals had to reserve vehicles ahead of time.

"We wanted to go driving so we put in for a car, but we didn't get one because there was a shortage," she said.

Instead of driving around the island, the Josefsons enjoyed the time they spent at the Clover Crest hotel.

"Every night the Clover Crest hired steel bands and they played music and we danced," Mildred recalled.

Mildred said she and Jerry dressed up every night at the hotel to enjoy dancing, something she said was common among couples in those days. She said men in those days had to learn how to dance in order to become popular with the ladies.

"We danced around the pool every night and other guests who didn't know us thought we were part of the entertainment," Mildred said.

Besides dancing the Josefsons said they also enjoyed hunting for lobster on the beach with the locals one evening. They said they also made a trip out to Sandy Point to do some swimming away from the rocky beach that was in front of their hotel at the time. No matter what the Josefsons did while visiting Saint Croix in 1957, they said all of the locals were extremely friendly, even more so than today.

"Wherever you walked and passed a native, they would say good morning," Jerry said. "Everyone was friendly," Mildred said.

The Josefsons said Saint Croix is, however, still a friendly place.

"Hospitality and extraordinary friendliness is still part of the Crucian way," Mildred said.

While visiting Saint Croix this week, the Josefsons enjoyed some of that hospitality while staying at the Pink Fancy Hotel in Christiansted. The 11 room, bed and breakfast-style hotel, national historical site, was recently purchased over the summer by Calvin Coolidge—a distant nephew of President Calvin Coolidge—and his wife Joan. The Josefsons said the Coolidges displayed so much friendliness, kindness and thoughtfulness during their stay that it helped make their visit to Saint Croix even more enjoyable.

Calvin Coolidge even drove the Josefsons for a tour of the island, taking them back to their honeymoon spot at the Clover Crest hotel.

"We had to cut through bush like we were in a jungle to get there," Jerry said about his visit to the old Clover Crest hotel on Wednesday.

Jerry said the Clover Crest is currently an abandoned building that is overgrown with brush. He said the swimming pool which was cut in the shape of a clover leaf was still on the property even though it was filled with dirty rainwater and leaves. He said there is also still an old sugar mill on the property.

After enjoying some time on Saint Croix and reminiscing about their honeymoon, the Josefsons will return to Staten Island on Saturday. Jerry a former New York attorney, is currently involved with real estate investment. Mildred, who paints 17th-century-style portraits using oils, is a retired public high school chemistry teacher. The Josefsons have three grown children—a daughter, Dr. Debbie Josefson, and two sons, Michael and Howard Josefson.

Even though the Josefsons will soon be leaving the tropical paradise of Saint Croix to return to New York, they will forever remember the fun times they spent on Saint Croix back in 1957, as well as the fun times they enjoyed during this week's visit.

"This is a very special place," Mildred said about the big island.

CHAPTER 50

Wrapping Things Up and Heading Home (Cal)

AT THE HEIGHT of my depression over the previously impending doom, we'd had to make a decision about having our girls and their significant others come to the island for Christmas. Of course, we wanted them to be with us. Melinda and David were self-sufficient, but we'd have to get flights for Sarah and Jorah, both UCLA graduate assistants living in poverty in Los Angeles. These flights (we were learning) quickly tripled in cost at the holidays. Thankfully, we put our financial strain at the time aside and brought them in "on scholarship." Setting aside two nice rooms for them didn't affect our cash flow; even at Christmas, we were only half-full.

The kids were scheduled to come in on the twenty-seventh and stay through New Year's Day. On the twenty-sixth, Melinda called and announced, "David and I entered into a domestic partnership today." They lived in Washington, DC, and this, apparently, is the Millennial version of getting married. It took some explaining on their part for us to understand the concept. They had been together for four years; we were happy for them.

"Come on down, and we'll celebrate." We'd been spared the cost of hosting a wedding, but I did wonder if I would ever get the chance to walk a daughter down the aisle. Not that important when you ponder it.

It was the best week of our time on the island. The kids helped us out with the other guests, leaving us all enough time to do the fun island stuff that visitors should do. We loved having them all together.

New Year's Eve brought an invitation for all of us to a big party at our very close neighbor Mona's stately home. Her house was so close that when she opened her bedroom windows to catch the morning sun, she looked over our courtyard and pool. She was known to host a hell of a party. Our mutual pals, the KraZi Stans, were on the planning committee, and everyone in Mona's in crowd was invited. We were honored to have made the list. Highlights were the food stations with all sorts of goodies and, of course, the rum drinks.

At the stroke of midnight, the KraZi Stans and a few accomplices, who had silently disappeared minutes before, flung open the storm shutters on Mona's third floor and unleashed a barrage of water balloons on the crowd standing in the courtyard below. All in good fun. My memory of that moment was looking directly at Joan as she held a plate of food and seeing her take a direct hit to the back of the head. It reminded me of the Zapruder film of the Kennedy assassination, the balloon exploding forward and engulfing her head with water.

I have a very bad habit of laughing hysterically at others' pain. While it really wasn't painful, it was a classic hit. She survived and even forgave the KraZi Stans. Everyone enjoyed the fleeting moment of teenage fun as 2007 arrived.

We could only chuckle when Sarah announced that, after getting back to LA, she and Jorah, who had seemed the perfect guy to us, were splitting up. I hadn't even received the Amex bill for their expenses at that point.

The Mount Vernon group arrived just the week before we were scheduled to close and leave the island. They were all great, understanding guests. I was ready for a blowout when we all took the last sunset sail. The rum punch flowed, and I overdid it. Joan found no humor in my behavior and had no sympathy for me when, on my return to the Pink Fancy, I dove into our pool fully clothed and with my cell phone in my pocket. When you've escaped a situation like we had found ourselves in, the pent-up stress comes out. Whoops.

January 17 was a joyous day. We had gone to closing the day prior. Hank had been paid off, and we had a very large cashier's check in our hands. Yes, we had lost some money on this adventure, but as I told most who asked how much, it was about equal to the price of a used Buick. It could have been a disaster.

The same movers who had unpacked us eight months earlier must have been scratching their heads when they refilled the container with all the same boxes they had unloaded before. They had now unpacked and repacked the personal items we'd brought to furnish our "spacious yet convenient" living quarters in the old schoolhouse building and one-butt kitchen. Even less furniture than we'd brought with us made the return trip.

If you want an exercise in downsizing, a boomerang move like ours will do. When we'd moved to Alexandria from Texas in 1992, we had a United Van Lines truck overloaded with, I recall, twenty-two thousand pounds. Think of that van with the bicycles tied on the back that you've passed on the interstate—that was us. Now we'd be shipping home about eleven thousand pounds, at least a ton less than had made its way to Saint Croix in June. This is not the least expensive method of downsizing, but it will cure you of having too much shit.

We called Jacobs for a ride to the airport. On the way, he claimed—in that wonderful baritone voice with the perfect diction that I loved hearing—that he was losing his best friend on the island. It brought some tears to my eyes, but I was sure that he had many other "best friends." We had been pals; he had shared his recipe for a Crucian pork-shoulder BBQ, teaching me how to brine the meat and then submerge thin slices of garlic deep into it, avoiding the bone.

That meat dish, along with the Crucian stuffing that Sarah Harvey had shared with me, were the staples of any meal we hosted at the Pink Fancy. Sarah was the aunt of NBA star Tim Duncan and had played a big role in his life. The walls of her restaurant were graced with paintings of the big man going to the hoop.

Sarah Harvey's Crucian Stuffing Recipe

Box of Instant Potatoes or real mashed potatoes rather whipped (we used the instant)

2 eggs beaten in to the potatoes sized to serve multiples of 12

Add tomato sauce for color bringing it to an orangish red

Scallions chopped, red bell pepper diced

Anna's Hot Sauce –pour in to taste (be careful but generous to bring in the Island zest)

Sugar or Equal to taste

One small box of raisans

Essence- ½ teaspoon

Mix in a flat cake pan greased with butter spoon smooth the top

Fork in a design if desired- cook until it becomes brown on top at 325 degrees

We had included Jacobs and his wife in an invitation to a large evening meal we prepared for the crew of the Roseway, the three-mast schooner that made its winter home in Christiansted Harbor. The crew had been our hotel guests a week earlier. The gesture of reaching out to a cab driver had made me his favorite, I believe. We never witnessed any real racial prejudice on the island, but the act of mixing the locals and the white tourists was not common, it seemed. I looked at it like inviting the celebrity doing voice-overs on the next Hollywood film. Jacobs was truly blessed with the pipes of God. If this book gets converted to audio, it would be an honor to have Jacobs be our narrator.

Joan and I boarded the American Airlines flight with our one-way tickets. I settled into a window seat, Joan beside me in an aisle seat. We lifted off to the east and made a sharp turn north. The plane tilted perfectly to give us a view of beautiful Christiansted Harbor. I pointed out the pink roof of the hotel and watched it disappear as we climbed out and headed toward Miami.

We'd touch down at Washington Reagan at 1:30 p.m. on a bright, sunny January day. The forty-seven-degree sunshine felt great.

We had survived the experience. As we've told many friends, when we landed, we had no car, no home, and no jobs, but no debt—and most of the cash we'd left with seven months earlier. It was truly a liberating feeling. Neither of us had ever experienced such a feeling of freedom, always having had some set of obligations, whether it had been to our jobs, our kids, the mortgage, or just the pace of life we all fall into.

We opened a search for the next chapter of our lives. At age fifty-five, realistically, we needed to find some type of work that would provide us health insurance, as Joan's breast cancer was still being treated and was an obvious preexisting condition. But other than that, we were free to go anywhere. We had tried to procure health insurance on the island when the coverage on the plan Joan had had through the Fairfax public-school system ran out. We were flatly denied because of her condition.

It is a scary thing to go without coverage. We had done it for the past seven months, and it had only added to the stress we were under.

We made the decision that we'd find the place we wanted to live before we thought about what we would do to solve the medical-insurance issue. Having lived in six states in our lives together, we had seen positives in all, but Virginia had been our favorite. The natural beauty of the northern Shenandoah Valley beckoned. But so did the Eastern Shore of Maryland, Charlottesville, and the Williamsburg area. Two weeks of considering the decision and imposing on friends kept leading us back to the Shenandoah Valley.

After considering properties high on the Blue Ridge, we wisely found an emerging active-adult community at Lake Frederick that was off to a fast start. The complication was that it appeared there were no spec homes, and we faced a six-month building process. This is not what you want to hear when you are living out of a suitcase, with all your other worldly goods due to show up in two weeks.

As we walked out of the sales office, having ruled out the building process, the salesperson finally came clean. There were two homes that were "possibly available." Most likely, these were from failed contracts, which were just starting to appear as the real estate crisis we all would experience from then until 2010 began to take hold. "Here are the keys. Go take a look," he said.

Joan was so tired of walking though homes, I couldn't get her out of the car after we ruled out a duplex on the first stop. The second sat on a freshly sodded lawn at a high point on a street with only six homes and some twenty vacant lots. It provided a view of the Blue Ridge mountains from the dinette and the deck we would later add.

I went in and thought, *This could work.* It took some prodding, but Joan summoned her last bit of energy and came in. As we later said many times, "This home has everything we need but nothing we don't need."

That was on a Thursday. We closed the following Friday, able to pay cash with the proceeds we had barely escaped the island with.

In this case, our ability to make a snap decision turned out to be positive. We have been in our home at Lake Frederick for coming up on eleven years. Joan says they are going to take us out feet first. Our moving days are behind us. We have seen the community struggle and then thrive as it became Trilogy Resort at Lake Frederick, a now-booming destination for active older adults just outside of the quaint towns of Front Royal and Winchester.

Our Caribbean adventure remains the biggest walk on the wild side we could have dreamed up. Things work out—or, at least, they did for us. I have always been lucky. Life has taught me that to be lucky, you must expect to be lucky. Optimism, which I had come close to losing forever on the island, may lead you to take on challenges that you could have avoided, but in the end, it is optimism that makes anticipating what is next in life enjoyable.

We may have been crazy to take this walk, but at least we had the guts to try.

The End

Appendix and Acknowledgments

OUR COVER PHOTO is by Steve Simonson. It appeared in the February 2001 edition of *Caribbean Life and Travel*.

The history of Mary Pomeroy and her connection to Saint Croix, Nisbitt Plantation on Nevis, and Mary's Boon on Saint Martin were taken from the website of Mary's Boon. We heard the stories while on the island, that website provided an interesting summary.

Fancy That –the poem that serves as a divider between parts 1 and 2 of the book was written by our good friend Sherel Horsley.

You'll also find a few old advertisements previous owners had run over the years, proclaiming the Pink Fancy the Jewel of the Caribbean. Take note that thirty years later, the pricing structure we could attract business at had not changed a heck of a lot!

Finally, there is the Christmas letter that Cal managed to create in 2006 soon after we had signed the contract to sell the Pink Fancy. In it, he was able to regain a bit of humor about the whole situation. It promised that we'd write a book about this experience, which at the time we planned to title, *I Just Want to Be Dry*. Cal must have said that four thousand times as he sweated through T-shirts, slaving daily to survive and serve as the hotel's cleaning-and-maintenance staff. Friends we sent it to claim it still makes them laugh ten years later.

We want to thank all those who listened to our stories over the past ten years and encouraged us to complete the book. Special thanks to the writers' club that Cal joined, to whom he presented portions of the manuscript over the past year and a half.

OCTOBER 1984 · PRICE $2.50

Esquire

Cal Coolidge and Joan Coolidge

American Express Presents

EXPRESSIONS

In This Issue

*The Pink Fancy,
St. Croix*

IN ST. CROIX: THE PINK FANCY

One discovers the historic Pink Fancy, a small, cozy inn, in the heart of Christiansted (on St. Croix, U.S. Virgin Islands).

Twelve double rooms, all with private bath, kitchenette, cable TV, telephone, ceiling fans and air-conditioning, surround a freshwater pool and provide for a quiet, comfortable stay. Shops, restaurants and watersports are within a five minute walk, and the beach is nearby.

Rates through December 15, are US$65-75 for a single and $75-90 for a double. From December 16 through April 16, 1993, a single costs $85-95, and a double $95-125. Complimentary continental breakfast is included.

For additional

information and reservations, contact your travel agent, American Express Representative* or call (800) 524-2045, toll-free from the U.S., or (809) 773-6448 from elsewhere. •

Christmas Letter 2006 from Cal and Joan

Temporarily serving 6 months to life on St. Croix

32 years together and this is our first Christmas letter. We have always tried to send a personal note along with the cards we send giving a small update and where we are, what is new and how the kids are doing (great).

This year provided events that require more than a few words, in fact 2006 for us is the subject of an upcoming book we just have to write.

The title for the cover is "I just want to be dry". It is the true story of a suburban couple that rather impulsively "follows the dream" of casting it all aside and buying a small hotel in the Caribbean.

What is wrong with that idea? Nothing, until you get past chapter 4. If you have read the Herman Wouk novel "Don't Stop the Carnival" you may wonder how we can tell this story and not be charged as plagiarists. All we can say is this is a work of non-fiction!

The book will be in development in early 2007. For the purposes of the Christmas letter you will have to be satisfied with the Chapter headings and an occasional comment.

I Just want to be Dry

Chapter 1 "Seeds of discontent"....where fed-up with life in the big city Joan threatens to just go buy a B & B in the Caribbean and hasn't decided if she'll tell Cal where it is!

Chapter 2 "The internet is a dangerous place"....where Cal decides a pre-emptive strike is in order, he'll find it first!

Chapter 3 "It's just a vacation"....we'll just take a look while we are there. Trouble brews for a couple that have moved quickly 5 times.

Chapter 4 "Hey it's easy, we get all the business we want"....where low occupancy numbers are easily explained away by pleasant little hostesses.

Chapter 5 "The thrill of the deal"....where Cal loses sight of whether the goal is making a good deal or just proving he can do it.

Chapter 6 "Ugly truths about insurance on a Caribbean island"....why people there "self-insure".

Chapter 7 "We are all-in baby".... The house sells and the move date is established.

Christmas Letter 2006 from Cal and Joan

Chapter 8 "You must be nuts"....what friends and neighbors really mean when they tell you this has always been their dream.

Chapter 9 "Arrival"....was that unsecured 60 foot mobile home always across the street?...When you first notice the neighborhood might be the 'hood!

Chapter 10 "Just sign here"....Going to closing in the Virgin Islands. Where documents waiving your right to a jury trial are presented routinely.

Chapter 11 "Is it always this hot?".... learning that "there is always a breeze" and "I never use my A/C" are directly related to the electric bill you are about to get.

Chapter 12 "Just how am I going to spend my $1000 today at the hardware store?"...what you wake up wondering after 3 weeks in an "historic property"

Chapter 13 "I just want to be dry"....the rainy season is only interrupted by periods of extreme tropical air. Cal sets the USVI record by going through 6 tee shirts by noon as he cleans rooms.

Chapter 14 "You just need to make it through one high season"....advice from surviving entrepreneurs. "When is that?" asks Cal. "Sometimes as early as the end of January through like April 1st"

Chapter 15 "The thrill of Grocery shopping"....one list, three stores, no food but lots of liquids.

Chapter 16 "Losing 10 grand a month getting ready for high season"....This is just not going to work dawns on Cal.

Chapter 17 "Fun stories about colorful characters"...they are all here because they aren't all there!

Chapter 18 "The Exit Strategy"....this could be a five year process

Chapter 19 "Prayers are answered"....the hot real estate market, dead in the states follows Cal and Joan to St. Croix. - Woody makes our day – Hardball costs money buyers learn.

Chapter 20 "Heading home, with lessons learned by having had the guts to try"....not to mention a book to write!

After the Storms of 2017

As THIS BOOK goes to print in October 2017 Saint Croix is recovering from the double whammy of Hurricanes Irma, which just gave the island a glancing blow, and Hurricane Maria which was a direct hit. In the days after Irma the people of Saint Croix rallied to become a lifeline for their fellow islanders on Saint Thomas and St John only to face a crushing blow from Hurricane Maria. Saint Croix will require all of our help to recover its destroyed infrastructure and properties. We have already made a significant contribution and are offering our home in Virginia to old friends on the island who may need shelter while their houses are repaired.

Charities we personally suggest helping include:

www.canebaycares.org whose founders are matching the first $200,000 contributed

www.cruzancowgirls.com which helps rescue homeless animals including horses on the island.

www.sunshinefoundationstx.org whose mission has been to support animal neglect and abuse on the island.

About the Authors

In 1973 Cal and Joan met in Bradley University physics class; not too long after, the two were married. Cal notably worked for more than twenty-six years in the defense industry before switching gears and moving into the financial world as a stockbroker and financial advisor. Along the way, Joan found her calling as a librarian and mother.

In 2006, the two decided to leave their hectic but stable jobs and seek adventure. They purchased and briefly operated a small hotel on the US Virgin Island of Saint Croix.

Cal and Joan are finally settled with their dog, Max, in the upper Shenandoah Valley of Virginia. They spend a good part of the year traveling, spending each February on Key West.

Joan is a keen reader of fictional mysteries while Cal's interests include travel and golf. Cal and Joan raised two impressive young women, Melinda and Sarah, their daughters.

10529713R00138

Made in the USA
Lexington, KY
27 September 2018